Inchie Quilts

nadine

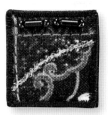

Located in Paducah, Kentucky, the American Quilter's Society (AQS) is dedicated to promoting the accomplishments of today's quilters. Through its publications and events, AQS strives to honor today's quiltmakers and their work and to inspire future creativity and innovation in quiltmaking.

EXECUTIVE EDITOR: ANDI MILAM REYNOLDS
SENIOR EDITOR: LINDA BAXTER LASCO
GRAPHIC DESIGN: ELAINE WILSON
COVER DESIGN: MICHAEL BUCKINGHAM
QUILT PHOTOGRAPHY: CHARLES R. LYNCH
HOW-TO PHOTOGRAPHY: NADINE RUGGLES

Additional copies of this book may be ordered from the American Quilter's Society, PO Box 3290, Paducah, KY 42002-3290, or online at www.AmericanQuilter.com.

Library of Congress Cataloging-in-Publication Data

Ruggles, Nadine.
  Inchie quilts / by Nadine Ruggles.
    p. cm.
  ISBN 978-1-57432-991-9
  1. Patchwork--Patterns. 2. Quilting--Patterns. I. Title.
  TT835.R85 2009
  746.46'041--dc22

                                    2009014068

American Quilter's Society
P. O. Box 3290 • Paducah, KY 42002-3290
www.AmericanQuilter.com

Dedication

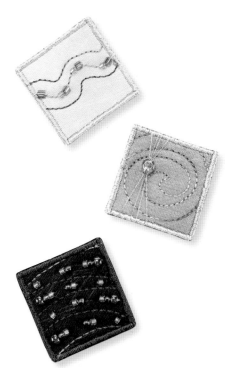

Dedicated to my Grandmama,

who took my little crafty bits of fabric and yarn, popsicle sticks,

shells and beads, salt dough, and cardboard,

and held them to her heart as the finest works of art.

And to my mother,

always my first editor, supporter, listener, friend.

She keeps telling me I really am a true artist.

I think maybe I finally believe.

Aknowledgments

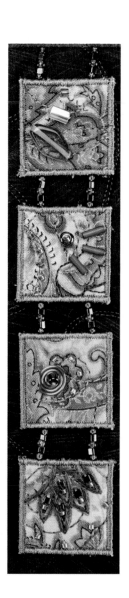

Grateful thanks to:

Weeks Dye Works for donating their beautiful hand overdyed embroidery flosses,

Hobbs Bonded Fibers for contributing Thermore® Ultra Thin Batting, and

RNK Distributing for donating Floriani Heat N Sta Fusible Light Fleece® batting.

To Carol Duffy of San Francisco Stitch Co., thank you ever so much for answering my last minute, super rushed design request with a "Yes!" It was such a pleasure working with you, and the INCHIE CHESS quilt truly sings, thanks to you.

Heartfelt thanks to Linda Lasco, Andi Reynolds, Elaine Wilson, and the whole AQS team. Thank you for believing in the large potential of such small works of art.

To my daughters, Erica and Erin, thank you a thousand times from the bottom of my heart for helping out and putting up with Mom's "all quilting, all the time" distraction and late or make-it-yourself dinners, not just for this book, but for the many previous years full of quilting obsessions. I love you both.

To my loving husband Eric, "Thank you" just doesn't say enough. Your love and support in this and everything mean more than I can say. I love you now and forever.

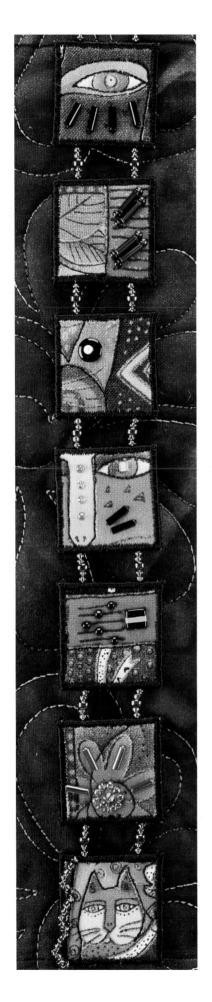

Table of Contents

Something More Than Just Patchwork

Inchies are 1" x 1" art squares made of paper or fabric and embellished with beads, fibers, crystals, wire, found objects, or anything you desire. I discovered Inchies sometime after the fabric postcard craze turned into the artist trading card craze, when my good friend Birgit at Patchcom in Shönaich, Germany, showed me a few fabric Inchies made by one of her customers. Evidently, fabric artists had begun making Inchies the same way they made fabric postcards and artist trading cards, with fabric, batting, and sometimes a stiffener, and a wide variety of stitchery and embellishments, then swapping Inchies with other fabric artists.

I thought, "A one inch canvas is so small. How can you make an interesting design in just one square inch of space?" and put it out of my head for a while. Later, I was designing a quilt for the New Quilts from an Old Favorite contest sponsored by The National Quilt Museum in Paducah, Kentucky. The theme block for the contest was Burgoyne Surrounded, a traditional block with many small squares. I was tossing around an idea that would include many small quilts

attached temporarily in some way to a larger background quilt; certain elements of the design could be rearranged for color and design options even after the quilt was finished.

Taking a break from the design process and some other ongoing projects, I decided to try making some Inchies just for fun. I did a little research on the Internet to see what was out there and tried to find a tutorial as a place to start. I found a few different tutorials, as well as many pictures, and loads of information about groups of quilters and fabric artists who were swapping Inchies. I made my first set of 48 Inchies and was instantly hooked on the whole process.

I showed my Inchies to a few quilting friends and the almost universal response was "Wow, cool! But what do you do with them?" During my research, I noticed that although quilters and fabric artists were making, swapping, and collecting Inchies, there weren't many display ideas being shared. What were people doing with all of these Inchies? Putting them in a box or in a folder? Making jewelry or what?

I thought about making a small, very simple quilt to display my Inchies. Then my two projects—the Inchies and the Burgoyne Surrounded quilt—suddenly juxtaposed in my head. Yes, I could make a very simple background quilt for this first set of Inchies, but I could take this idea one step further and integrate the Inchies into a larger quilt design for the Burgoyne Surrounded quilt as well! I could attach the Inchies with Velcro so that they'd be movable for a color play type of quilt. More ideas for quilt designs featuring Inchies followed, almost faster than I could write them down.

Small squares in patchwork blocks and quilt designs have always held a certain fascination for me; Chain of Squares is one of my favorite border designs and has found its way into several of my pre-Inchie quilts. There's just something about a group of squares that's rhythmic and balanced, yet interesting and attractive.

Likewise, I'd been collecting beads and other small embellishment materials for years, though I didn't always have a solid plan for incorporating them into quilted projects. Small packages of beads, bead and fiber mixes, tiny charms, buttons, laces, trims, crystals, and a variety of

found objects constantly found their way into my stash, awaiting the perfect use.

Inchies combine these small squares with fabulous embellishments to create beautiful fabric art with depth, detail, and textural interest. Inchies can be incorporated into traditional, contemporary, and art style quilts as an integral part of the design. Inchie quilts invite the viewer in. At first glance, you see the overall quilt design, but as you look closely, you see that the squares are something more than just patchwork. Look even more closely, and more and more intricate detail is revealed. You want to take your time and study each unique Inchie on the quilt.

Inchie Quilts is the answer to the "Well, Inchies are cool, but what do you do with them?" question! To get started making your own Inchie quilts, read through the Tools and Supplies, Fabric Choices for Inchies, and Basic Inchie Instructions sections of this book, select your favorite Inchie quilt, and gather your tools, materials, and embellishments. Visit **www.InchieQuilts. com** to interact with other Inchie quilters, find tutorials and technical support, download bonus files for this book, and see even more Inchie quilts! Just dive in, and have fun!

Tools and Supplies

Having the all tools you need on hand will make the Inchie process easier and more enjoyable. In addition to the basic supplies that you use for general quiltmaking, there are some special tools and supplies you'll need to make Inchie quilts. Some are necessary for ease of construction, others are simply "nice to have," and some are only needed for certain techniques.

➡ The following are in the "necessary" category. **A sewing machine with zigzag stitch** capability is a must for edge stitching Inchies.

➡ **Rulers with very thin lines in a smaller format** like 4" x 8" or 3" x 9" are best for cutting Inchies.

➡ Some combinations of **stiffener and filler** that work are shown in the following chart. Experiment with other combinations. Look for materials that will combine to produce Inchies that are fairly thin and a little stiff, but still easy to sew through by hand when embellishing.

➡ **A low-loft, polyester batting** is best for Inchie quilts. Look for a batting that is thin and doesn't shrink.

➡ **A Teflon® pressing sheet** is necessary if your stiffener is double-sided fusible material.

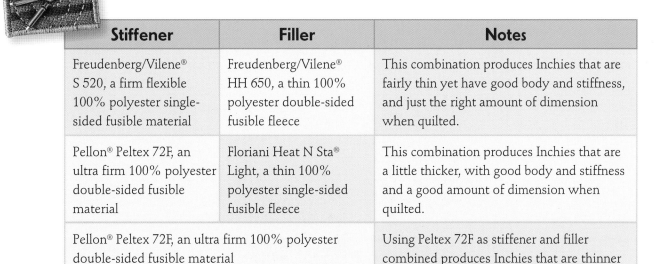

Stiffener	Filler	Notes
Freudenberg/Vilene® S 520, a firm flexible 100% polyester single-sided fusible material	Freudenberg/Vilene® HH 650, a thin 100% polyester double-sided fusible fleece	This combination produces Inchies that are fairly thin yet have good body and stiffness, and just the right amount of dimension when quilted.
Pellon® Peltex 72F, an ultra firm 100% polyester double-sided fusible material	Floriani Heat N Sta® Light, a thin 100% polyester single-sided fusible fleece	This combination produces Inchies that are a little thicker, with good body and stiffness and a good amount of dimension when quilted.
Pellon® Peltex 72F, an ultra firm 100% polyester double-sided fusible material		Using Peltex 72F as stiffener and filler combined produces Inchies that are thinner than other combinations and don't have as much dimension when quilted.

➡ Have a variety of **hand and machine needles:**

○ Use a Microtex/Sharp needle in a size appropriate for the thread you choose for quilting or couching on Inchies.

○ Use a size 10 Microtex/Sharp needle when edge-stitching Inchies. Try different brands; the Klassé brand seems to produce a slightly better edge stitch for me.

○ Use a size 10 straw needle for beading. True beading needles are too thin to go through the Inchies without bending or breaking.

○ Use a size 7 crewel needle for embroidery floss embellishments and larger sizes as necessary for larger or specialty fibers.

○ Use a size 24 or 26 chenille needle for silk ribbon embroidery embellishments.

○ Have an assortment of other handwork needles on hand. Sometimes, you just use whatever needle does the job.

➡ Use various types of **needle threaders** to make needle threading easier.

➡ Many different **threads** can be used for Inchies; here are the ones you'll definitely want to have on hand:

○ Anything goes for quilting and couching. Experiment with various colors, types, and weights of thread including cotton, rayon, and polyester.

○ Use 40-wt. rayon for edge stitching. This won't add too much bulk and usually comes in a wide array of colors.

○ You can also use 50-wt. cotton thread for edge-stitching. It adds a bit more bulk to the edges making them slightly bigger, which can be a disadvantage for quilt designs that require the Inchies to sit right next to each other and fit into a fixed space. Look for a thinner 50-wt. thread like the Aurifil brand.

○ Use 60-wt. cotton or other bobbin-weight thread in the bobbin to avoid thread buildup on the backs and edges.

○ Use a beading thread like Nymo D or C-Lon D for beaded embellishments. Use whatever color looks best with your fabric and bead combination.

➡ Use **finger cots** to help you grip the needle when adding embellishments to Inchies.

➡ It's best to have a variety of **scissors and thread snips** on hand for different tasks:

○ Choose a pair of very sharp **embroidery scissors** to cut beading thread, snip sewing threads, and clean up the edges.

○ Use a pair of **curved thread snips** to trim threads close to the Inchie sandwich.

➡ A selection of **permanent fabric markers**, like Pigma® Micron® pens, Sharpie® permanent markers, or Tsukineko® Fabrico® markers, will be handy to "dye" any bits of fabric or batting on the Inchies that are not covered by the edge stitching.

➡ Go crazy with **embellishments!** More is better. Just keep the small scale of Inchies in mind. If you intend to use fusible tape to attach the Inchies, be sure that the embellishments you choose won't be damaged by the heat from the iron.

○ Look for **bead mixes** with a large variety of small beads. Purchase good quality beads and check for colorfastness if in doubt by rinsing the beads in water. Some low quality beads are painted and the color can transfer or bleed to your fabric when you fuse fasteners to the Inchies.

○ Experiment with other materials like fibers, colored copper wire, hot-fix crystals, found items, small buttons, charms, hand-dyed embroidery floss and silk ribbon, fusible ribbon, fusible braid and trim, grommets, brads, and other small-scale scrapbooking items. The sky's the limit! Check for colorfastness on hand-dyed embellishments and prewash if necessary.

➡ Good quality **lighting** is a necessity, especially for edge stitching and embellishing Inchies.

➡ You'll need a variety of items to **attach your Inchies to the quilt:**

○ Use **fabric glue** to permanently attach Inchies to the quilt. Glue should be permanent and able to withstand washing.

○ Use **Velcro® brand Fabric Fusion® tape** to attach Inchies to quilts so that they can be rearranged.

○ Use a bristled **pressing cloth** (like that used to press velvet or velveteen) or a thick folded towel as a pad under Inchies to protect beads and other embellishments when fusing the hook side of Velcro to the back of the Inchies.

○ Use a **cotton pressing cloth** to protect the quilt and the Velcro when fusing the loop side of Velcro to the quilt.

➡ The following items are useful to have:

○ Use the **InchieSee Viewer Tool** to preview fabrics to see how they'll look when

cut into Inchies (see Resources, page 78).

○ Use the **InchieDo Ruler** to cut Inchies perfectly straight and square. The ruler has very thin lines with open spaces at the corners so you can see exactly where to cut (see Resources, page 78).

○ A **beading cloth** or a scrap of a Martex® Vellux® blanket keeps beads and other embellishments from bouncing or rolling off the table.

○ A pair of **surgical quality tweezers** helps with selecting and placing beads and crystals and for holding threads to trim close to the Inchies and the quilt.

○ **Bead trays** and a **bead scoop** are both worthy additions to your beading supplies.

○ Use a **Quilter's BlockButler®** design wall to temporarily display Inchies during construction. It helps to see what types and styles of embellishments you've already done.

➡ These items are needed for certain types of embellishments:

○ A **hole cutter** and **eyelet** or **grommet setter** to set eyelets or grommets.

○ A **hot-fix crystal heat setter** for applying hot-fix crystals.

○ An **X-Acto® knife** to cut slits in Inchies to apply brads.

○ **Round-nosed pliers** or a **wire wrapping jig** and **wire cutters** to cut and form colored copper wire.

○ A **mini iron** to affix fusible ribbon and trim.

Fabric Choices for Inchies

When you are choosing fabrics for Inchies almost anything goes. In a colorwash style where you use batiks, mostly solids, or tone-on-tone fabrics, your embellishments and quilting take center stage and you create the design. When you use multicolor prints, the fabric print becomes the main design element and you accent the design with your quilting and embellishments.

Choosing a medium-to-large print with many different design elements and colors can sometimes produce Inchies that look as if they were made from two or more different fabrics. The INCHIE ART GALLERY quilt (page 11) is a great example of this effect. The Inchies were all made from the fabric shown in figure 1. Embellishments were chosen to accentuate the differences in colors and design elements between the four "sets" of Inchies.

Checks, plaids, and obvious or large stripes present a special challenge. If you use these types of prints, be sure to cut the Inchies straight, in line with the stripes, or there will be the illusion that the Inchies are not actually square. This does not mean that you should not use these fabrics, and in fact, if you are looking for a special effect, by all means experiment with them. But be aware of the difficulties they present.

Experiment with many different fabrics and take the InchieSee Viewer Tool with you to the quilt shop when you plan to buy. You'll be able to audition fabrics to see what a 1" x 1" square

FIG. 1.

will look like (fig. 2). You can also cut a chunk out of the fabric and cut 1" x 1" squares from it to audition as well, without actually making an Inchie sandwich with filler, stiffener, and backing.

Whatever print you choose, try to stay away from fabrics that are very loosely woven, as the edge stitching will be more difficult and won't look as smooth and finished. Batik fabrics edge stitch wonderfully, as do most of the higher quality quilting cottons, but fabrics with a low thread count are not good choices. Prewash Inchie fabrics to remove sizing so that fusible materials stick better.

FIG. 2.

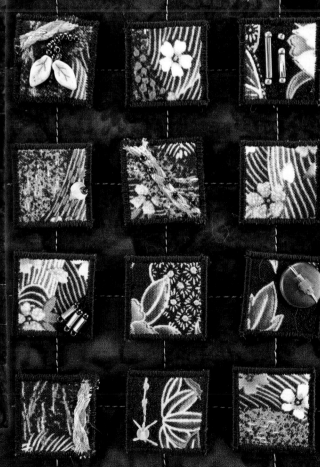

THE INCHIE ART GALLERY quilt and detail (right)

Basic Inchie Instructions

Making a Sandwich

For single-sided fusible stiffener, place the backing fabric wrong side up on an ironing board and lay the stiffener on top, shiny side down. (For double-sided fusible stiffener, lay the stiffener on a Teflon pressing sheet on the ironing board, and place the backing fabric right side up on the stiffener.)

Fuse the stiffener and backing fabric layers together using a hot iron with steam for about 15 seconds, slightly overlapping the pressed areas until completely fused. (For double-sided stiffener, let cool, turn over and remove the Teflon pressing sheet.) Place the filler on top of the

FIG. 1.

stiffener (if using single-sided filler, position the filler with the fusible side up) and lay the Inchie fabric on top, right side facing up (fig. 1).

For colorwash fabric Inchies, place the fabric squares next to each other (fig. 2) with no space between them.

Carefully lay a pressing cloth over the layers. Fuse the layers using a hot iron with steam for about 15 seconds, overlapping the pressed areas until completely fused.

Hold the iron up slightly so that the soleplate is just touching the fabric, preventing the full weight of the iron from sitting on the sandwich. You want the steam and heat to penetrate all the layers without letting the weight of the iron flatten all the puff out of the filler.

FIG. 2.

Quilting and Couching for Texture

I use a Clover® Hera™ marker and a ruler to mark lines on the Inchie sandwich when making colorwash Inchies, dividing the fabric pieces into 1¼" squares. The lines provide a guide for machine quilting patterns.

Add quilted details and designs to the Inchie sandwich for texture and to anchor the layers firmly together. Reduce the top tension on your machine. Use a 60-wt. or bobbin thread that coordinates with your backing fabric. Choose a Microtex/Sharp needle in a size that works well with the type of top thread you are using.

Use a smaller stitch length for quilting on the sandwich so that when the Inchies are cut apart later, the quilting stitches are less likely to come apart at the edges. Test thread combinations, colors, stitches, and tension settings on a separate test sandwich made with the same fabrics, filler, and stiffener to see what looks best and works well.

Try some free-motion quilting or decorative machine stitches. Experiment with variegated or other specialty threads. For one-fabric Inchies, quilt on the design lines of the fabric (fig. 3) or use the fabric design as the background for your own free-motion designs. Aim for at least two lines of quilting on each Inchie to keep the layers from shifting when edge stitching.

If you're making colorwash Inchies, try the quilting patterns included on page 37 as inspiration. Don't worry about whether your stitching is perfect. Embellishments can hide a multitude of wobbles, bumps, jagged edges, and not-so-smooth curves!

Consider couching special trims or fibers, stitching over fabric bits, Angelina® fiber, or other machine-friendly embellishments. If you intend to attach the Inchies to your quilt using fusible Velcro, any embellishments need to be iron- and heat-safe. Anything goes here; as long as you can sew through it or over it and cut it with a rotary cutter, it's fair game for Inchies!

Tip! Don't have just the right color thread for quilting or edging? Use a thread that's one or two shades lighter, darker, or toward another color.

Colorwash Inchie Quilting Designs

The area inside the solid line measures 1¼" x 1¼". The dashed line surrounds the actual Inchie design space of 1" x 1" (fig. 4, page 14). These designs are meant for inspiration to give you a starting point when you are quilting a sandwich of colorwash Inchies. The designs should be fairly small in scale, in keeping with the diminutive nature of Inchies.

FIG. 3.

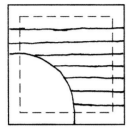 

FIG. 4. Colorwash Inchie Quilting design samples. See more designs on page 37.

The quilting designs have beginning and ending points that are always outside the Inchie design area. Some designs can be quilted in one continuous line. Others are made of multiple lines and you'll need to "travel" outside the design area in the area between the squares to get from one line to the next.

Cutting It Up

There are two methods to cut individual Inchies.

METHOD 1: Totally Random!

Hold the ruler firmly and cut 1" strips from the sandwich. Don't let the ruler slip! Cut 1" x 1" squares from the strip. Be surprised when you see the design on each unique Inchie!

METHOD 2: Picky and Choosy!

Cut 1" strips from the sandwich. Use the InchieSee Viewer Tool or a ruler to isolate a portion of the design. Center that portion on the ½" markings on the ruler and cut one side of the Inchie. Turn the strip 180 degrees, align the edge with the 1" mark, and cut the opposite side.

Note that if you plan to be picky and choosy, it's a good idea to make your Inchie sandwich at least 1¼" larger in each direction than called for in the project instructions.

Cut all the Inchies needed for your project all at once, being careful to keep them square with 90-degree corners. If you're using a regular rotary ruler, opt for one that has really thin lines, or use the half- or quarter-inch markings (if they are thinner lines) to measure and cut your Inchies (fig. 5).

The InchieDo Ruler (fig. 6) has thin dashed lines with open corners to make it easier to keep things on the straight and square while cutting.

On the Edge

To finish the edges, choose a thread color that coordinates with your Inchies and your project. It's best to choose a thread color slightly darker in value than your Inchie fabric.

Use an open-toed embroidery foot for the best visibility. Position the needle as far to the right as possible on your machine so that more of the Inchie is under the foot and connecting with the feed dogs. Leave a space equivalent to about two needle widths between the right edge of the Inchie sandwich and the inner edge of the open-toed foot (fig. 7). Use a new needle for edge stitching each set of Inchies. If it's a large set with many Inchies, change to a new needle halfway through. A new needle can make a huge difference in the quality of the edge stitching.

Reduce the upper thread tension so that the top thread wraps around the edge all the way to the back and the bottom thread doesn't show on the top or edge. Using one of the scraps cut away from the Inchie sandwich, experiment with your machine settings to get the best edge stitch.

With a very narrow zigzag stitch and a short stitch length, sew along the edge of the sandwich, with the needle going into the sandwich on the left swing of the needle and off the edge of the sandwich on the right swing.

If you can see the bobbin thread on the side of the sandwich after stitching, reduce the top thread tension a little more, or thread the bobbin thread through the "finger" or "pig's tail" on the bobbin case, should your machine be so equipped. Adjust the stitch width and the top tension until the edge stitch is about 1/16" wide and the top thread wraps around the edge.

Now adjust the stitch length for complete coverage. Stitches should be very dense and close together so that none of the fabric is showing between the stitches, but not so close that the stitches pile up and make a bump in the edge stitching and cause the machine to jam up on the bump. There are two methods of determining the correct stitch length.

METHOD 1: Count the Stitches!

Mark the edge of a scrap Inchie sandwich with two lines, 1/4" apart (fig. 8).

Starting before the first line, stitch along the edge of the Inchie. Begin counting the stitches when the needle reaches the first line and continue counting until the needle passes the second line. Count each time the needle goes down as one stitch. Aim for 24 to 28 stitches between the lines with good coverage. If you have fewer stitches, shorten the stitch length and try again.

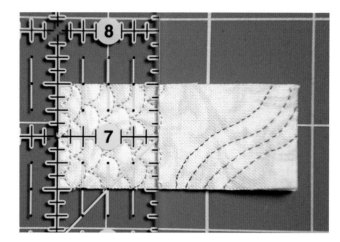

FIG. 5.

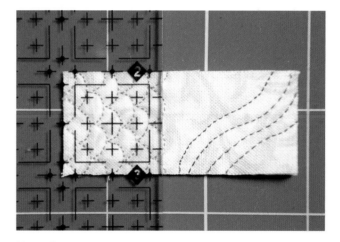

FIG. 6.

FIG. 7.

FIG. 8.

If you have more stitches, but the stitches aren't piling up, this is fine, too.

METHOD 2: Pile Up and Back Off!

Set your machine for a very short stitch length and test the edge stitch. Keep shortening the stitch length by a couple of levels before each test until there is no fabric showing between the stitches. If you shorten the stitch length too far and the stitches start piling up on each other, lengthen the stitches by one setting and test again.

Machine settings are highly variable. Experimentation is a must to get the right edge-stitch combination of tension and stitch width and length for each Inchie project.

Edge Stitching Sequence

Once you have determined the best machine settings, start in the middle of one side, holding the threads as you begin. Stitch to the corner, slowing down as you get closer, and stitch all the way off of the edge with that last stitch (fig. 9).

Tip! If your machine will save changes to stitch settings, use one stitch as the edge stitch and another as the "tie off" stitch, so that you can quickly switch between the two.

Stop stitching with the needle down on the right side of the Inchie, lift the presser foot slightly, and carefully turn the Inchie 90 degrees counterclockwise. Do not pull the corner of the Inchie away from the needle or pick it up off of the machine bed. Position it so that the very top of the corner is right next to and touching the needle.

Lower the presser foot and slowly begin stitching again, making sure that the Inchie stays straight and moves freely through the machine. Continue stitching in this manner until you reach the third side of the Inchie. Pause for a moment to trim the starting threads close to the Inchie. Continue on until you come around to the first side where you started and overlap the first stitches by a few stitches.

To end the edge stitching securely, set the machine for a very short straight stitch, with the needle positioned directly over the left side of the edge stitching. Make five or six small straight stitches to tie off the threads securely and virtually invisibly. Trim the threads close to the Inchie.

Touching It Up

Little bits of fabric and thread can often poke through the edge stitching despite the most care-

FIG. 9.

ful edging technique. Snip off any "pokies" very carefully, as close as possible without damaging the edge stitching. If there is any of the fabric or filler showing at the corners or on the edges, use a permanent fabric marker in a shade that closely matches your thread color to "dye" the offending bits. No one will ever know your secret.

Your Inchies are now ready to embellish! (See Embellishment Techniques, pages 21–32.)

Making Them Stick

Inchies can be fastened to a quilt with fusible Velcro tape, fabric glue, or bead links. How do you decide which attachment method to use?

For most quilts, glue is probably the best choice, being the easiest and most economical.

If you'd like to be able to rearrange the Inchies on the quilt, or even switch them out for a completely different set of Inchies, use Velcro. Inchies attached with Velcro will stick out farther from the quilt due to the thickness of the Velcro, which adds even more dimension to the quilt design. You can use fabric glue to attach the Velcro to the backs of any Inchies that might be damaged by high heat from the iron.

If you plan to add Inchie fringe to the bottom edge of the quilt, bead links are likely the best attachment method. Bead links leave the Inchies hanging free, though they are permanently attached.

Using Fabric Glue

Lay out the Inchies on the quilt as desired. Have a paper towel and a cup or glass handy to hold the paintbrush. Working with one Inchie at a time, use a small paintbrush to paint a small to medium amount of glue on the back of each Inchie, keeping the glue away from the very edges. Do not hold the Inchie over the quilt when applying the glue!

Carefully turn the Inchie over and position it on the quilt. Press gently into place to spread the glue slightly. Repeat for the remaining Inchies. Let dry overnight or according to glue manufacturer's instructions.

Using Velcro® brand Fabric Fusion™ tape

Working with just the hook side of the Velcro, cut a ¾" piece for each Inchie. Repeat with the loop side of the Velcro. To fuse the loop side of the Velcro to the quilt, lay the quilt on an ironing board, peel the release paper from the back of the Velcro, and press into position. The adhesive will stick temporarily. Apply a small number of pieces to the quilt in a manageable area, then turn the quilt over so that the backing is facing up and the Velcro is underneath the quilt.

Lay a cotton pressing cloth over the area to be fused. With the iron set on high heat and full steam, fuse the Velcro to the quilt for 60 seconds. A little pressure against the quilt from the iron is okay when fusing. Lift the iron after 60 seconds and move to the next area to be fused. Keep the pressing cloth between the iron and the quilt. When all of the Velcro pieces in the area have been fused, turn the quilt back over, and continue to apply Velcro pieces. Repeat the process until all of the Velcro has been fused to the quilt.

After the quilt has cooled completely, check the Velcro pieces to make sure they are bonded well to the quilt. If any are loose, fuse the area again with high heat and full steam for another 60 seconds. Repeat this process until the Velcro pieces are securely bonded.

Look over all of your Inchies for any that have embellishments that could be damaged by high heat. Apply glue to the backs of these Inchies and affix the hook side of the Velcro. Press and hold the Velcro in place for a minute or so, depending on how fast the glue sets. Let the glue dry completely, then check the adhesion carefully; if needed, reapply glue.

Work with as many heat-safe Inchies as will fit side by side under the iron; 12 is a good number to try. Remove the release paper from the hook side and press each piece to the back of an Inchie. Lay the Inchies Velcro side up on a bristled pressing cloth or folded towel. Cover the Inchies with a cotton pressing cloth. Set the iron on high heat and full steam, and fuse the Velcro to the backs of the Inchies for 60 seconds. Try not to put too much pressure or weight on the Inchies with the iron so as not to damage the Velcro with the heat and weight of the iron.

After fusing, fold the bristled pressing cloth or towel up over the Inchies, and flip the whole thing over quickly with the Inchies inside. Uncover the Inchies, place a towel over the Inchies and apply pressure with your hands for 30 to 60 seconds until the Inchies are slightly cool. When they are completely cool, check to make sure the Velcro is bonded well to the backs. If needed, repeat the fusing process for any pieces that are not well bonded.

When both the quilt and the Inchies are completely cool, fasten the Inchies to the quilt. Position each Inchie as desired and gently press into place. When you are satisfied with the placement of all the Inchies, use your fingers to "smoosh" each one into place by moving it up and down and side to side to set the hook side of the Velcro firmly into the loops.

To remove Inchies from the quilt, grasp firmly on a straight edge, not a corner, and pull straight down or to the side while holding the quilt firmly with your free hand. The corners are the weakest part of the Velcro/fabric bond and pulling the Inchies off diagonally could loosen the bond.

Making Bead Links

To attach Inchies with bead links, first arrange the Inchies as desired on the quilt. You will link the Inchies together starting at the bottom Inchie and working upwards on one side, attaching the string of Inchies to the quilt, then working back down the other side of the string. The needle should always travel between the stiffener and the batting only so that the beading thread does not show on the front.

You can use any combination of beads that measures about ½" between the Inchies, as long as the sequence and number of beads is consistent throughout the string of Inchies.

Step 1. Working from the back of the Inchies, go in at A, and come out at B. Point B should be at the side edge of the Inchie. Pass the needle and thread through two seed beads, one larger bead, and two more seed beads.

Step 2. Insert the needle into the next Inchie in the string at point C. Come out at D on the back. Be sure that points B and C line up and are the same distance from the edges so that the Inchies and links hang straight.

Go in again at E and repeat steps 1 & 2 to link all the Inchies together (fig. 10).

To attach the linked Inchies to the quilt, after completing a step 2, pass the needle and thread through the top fabric and batting of the quilt for about ½". Be sure that the Inchies will hang correctly when you attach them to the quilt (fig. 11).

Pass the needle and thread through the same number of beads that you've used for the other links. Insert the needle into the top Inchie in the string at point A and come out at B.

Continue in the same manner to link the Inchies together. Tie off the thread on the back of the bottom Inchie in the string.

To attach Inchies to the edge of the quilt as a fringe, you'll use a similar method, working from top to bottom, instead of bottom to top, working from the back of the quilt.

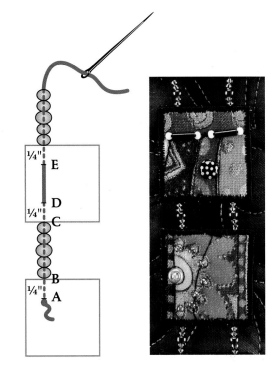

FIG. 10.

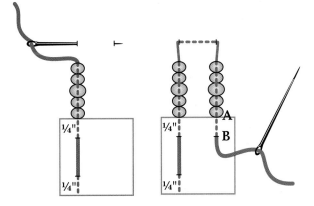

FIG. 11.

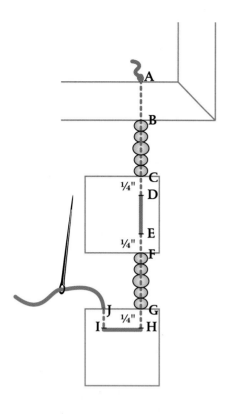

Arrange the Inchies at the edge of the quilt as desired, spacing them about ¼"–½" apart. Mark the Inchie placement on the quilt edge.

Insert the needle into the fabric behind the quilt binding at A and come out at B. Pass the needle and thread through two seed beads, one larger bead, and two more seed beads. Go in to the edge of the top Inchie of the fringe at C and come out at D on the back of the Inchie.

Insert the needle into the back of the Inchie at point E and come out at F on the edge. Pass the needle and thread through the same number of beads that you've used for the other links and insert the needle into point G on the next Inchie in the string.

Be sure that points F and G line up and are the same distance from the edges of the Inchies so that the Inchies and links hang straight.

Continue adding Inchies in this manner until you reach the last one in the string. Come out at H, go in at I, and come out at J. Add beads and continue in the same manner to link the Inchies in the string together.

When you reach the binding, guide the needle through the edge of the binding and come out at the point where the next Inchie string will be added. Add another string in the same manner. After the last string has been added to the edge of the quilt, tie off the thread on the back of the quilt close to the inside edge of the binding.

Quilt Care

Inchie quilts are made for the wall and therefore will probably only need an occasional gentle spot cleaning or shaking out to remove dust. Should a full wet cleaning be necessary, remove any Inchies if they are attached with Velcro. The quilt can then be washed and dried just as you care for other quilts, either by hand or machine.

If you must wash a quilt with glued or bead-linked Inchies on it, choose a mild soap and hand wash carefully in cool water. Rinse thoroughly and press the quilt gently between two towels to remove the excess water. Reshape and lay it flat on a towel to dry, flattening the Inchies if they have curled at the corners.

Embellishment Techniques

L et's get something straight from the beginning: there are no ugly Inchies. Perfection is neither desired nor required. When you look at an Inchie you've just quilted and wonder, "What the heck was I doing?", don't stress; this is where embellishments come in. Add fibers or beads, or both, and the "not so perfect" is beautiful!

Embellishments on Inchies can be as simple or as complex as you like. Using a variety of different materials, colors, styles, and scales will add depth and textural interest to your Inchies.

Here are some basic embellishment stitches and techniques to get you started.

Bead It

To add beads, use a doubled strand of nylon beading thread. Nymo® and C-Lon® threads both have some stretch, so pre-stretch the thread before using. Cut a 24"–30" strand at an angle for easier threading and stretch it firmly between your hands. Thread the needle, doubling the thread, and knotting the ends together as shown (fig. 1). Trim the threads to ⅛" below the knot.

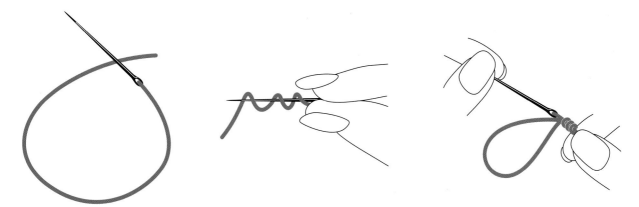

FIG. 1. Hold the thread ends behind and against the needle. Wrap the thread around the needle two or three times and pull tight. Hold the wrapped threads firmly between your thumb and forefinger and pull the needle and thread all the way through until a knot is formed at the end of the threads. A smaller knot is better, so try to only use two wraps of the thread if it will anchor the thread sufficiently.

Beginning and Ending Stitches

Take the first stitch through the backing fabric only (fig. 2), positioning the knot toward the middle. Keeping the threads and knots on the back of the Inchies flat as possible will help you later when you are attaching the Inchies to your quilt.

To end, take a couple of small stitches and then make a flat knot (fig. 3).

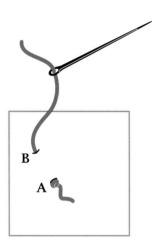

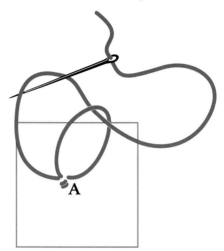

FIG. 2. Go in at A, toward the middle of the Inchie, and come out at B, traveling under the backing fabric layer only.

FIG. 3. Go in at A, toward the middle of the Inchie, and take two very small stitches close together, traveling under the backing fabric layer only. Make a third stitch near the first two, leaving a loop. Pass the needle through the loop and through the second loop made by the thread. Pull tight to make a knot. Trim threads to ⅛" from the knot.

Scattered Seeds

A scattering of single seed beads is delicate and interesting. Use any size seed beads or other small single beads of a similar size to make Scattered Seeds (fig. 4).

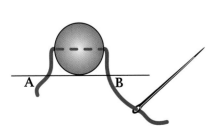

FIG. 4. Come up through the Inchie at A. Pass needle and thread through seed bead and go down at B, exactly one bead width from point A. If the distance from A to B is too long or too short, the bead will not stand up on the fabric.

Triple Treat

Stacking beads together gives a more textured look. Stack three size 11 seed beads or other small beads of a similar size to work Triple Treat (fig. 5).

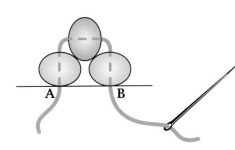

FIG. 5. Come up through the Inchie at A. Pass needle and thread through three seed beads and go down at B, exactly one bead width from point A. The bottom beads will lie flat against the fabric and the top bead will stand up on top of the other two.

Seed Spots

Use this stitch to anchor large beads, sequins, charms, tiny buttons, and found objects with a hole. Use size 11 seed beads to anchor larger, size 6 seed beads and other items to work Seed Spots (fig. 6).

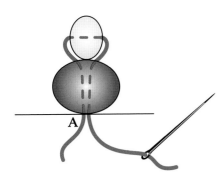

FIG. 6. Come up through the Inchie at A. Pass needle and thread through the larger bead and then through the seed bead. Pass needle and thread back through the larger bead and down through the Inchie very close to, but not right at, A. Pull thread tight and the seed bead will stand on top of the larger bead.

Continuous Curves

Use seed beads in multiples to create continuous curves. Draw a curved line if necessary or follow a line of quilting. Use size 11 seed beads to make curves as shown (fig. 7).

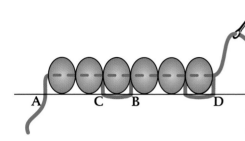

FIG. 7. Come up through the Inchie on the curved line at A. Pass needle and thread through three seed beads and go down at B. Come back up at C and pass the needle and thread through the last bead again, then through three more seed beads, and go down at D. Repeat to cover the entire curved line.

Bugle Bead Bars

Bugle beads require a bit of special handling as the ends can be quite sharp. Combine bugle beads with a seed bead at each end to prevent the sharp ends from cutting the beading thread. If you use bugle beads by themselves, use an additional strand of thread. Use a size 11 seed bead at each end of a size 5 or smaller bugle bead to make Bugle Bead Bars (fig. 8).

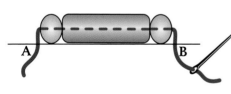

FIG. 8. Come up through the Inchie at A. Pass needle and thread through one seed bead, one bugle bead, and one more seed bead. Lay the beads down on the Inchie and use the needle to snug the beads up against the thread starting at point A. Go down at B, right at the end of the three beads.

Dangles

Strings of beads that dangle from an Inchie add movement and interest. Keep the final destination and direction of the Inchie in mind as it can affect the placement of the Dangles. Use seed beads for the main part of the dangle and add a larger, more interesting bead on the end (fig. 9).

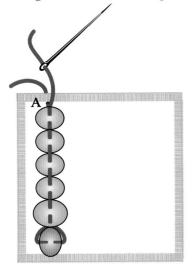

FIG. 9. Come up through the Inchie at A. Pass needle and thread through four or more seed beads, depending on how long the Dangle should be. Add a larger bead and one more seed bead. Pass the needle and thread back through the larger bead and all the seed beads above it. Go back through the Inchie close to, but not right at, A. Pull tight to bring all the beads together, but leave enough slack in the beading thread so that the Dangle lies down against the Inchie instead of standing out from it.

Embroider It

Small embroidered details will add a lot of depth and texture. Regular six-strand embroidery floss works well, though this is a great place to experiment with hand-dyed flosses. The floss should be separated into strands, and only 1–3 strands used at a time. Separate strands one at a time. Cut a length of floss and while holding one end grasp a single strand and pull it straight out from the others. Shake to straighten the remaining strands.

Thread your needle and tie a knot using the same knotting technique that you used for beading thread (page 21). Use the same beginning and ending techniques as for beading thread (page 22).

Colonial Knots

Use Colonial Knots anywhere you would a seed bead or in combination with seed beads (fig. 10). They're about the same size.

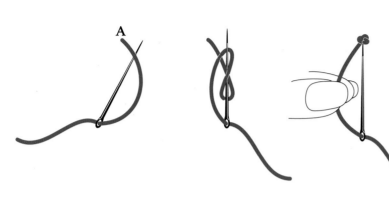 

FIG. 10. Come up through the Inchie at A and work the needle around under the thread. Grasp the embroidery thread close to the Inchie and wrap the thread around the needle in a figure eight as shown. Insert the needle close to A, but not exactly in the same spot, and pull the figure eight knot tight around the needle and down, so that it's flush on the surface of the Inchie. Pull the needle all the way through the Inchie while still holding the thread taut around the needle, then pull the thread until the knot is formed. Leave the knot a bit loose for best effect.

Beaded Cross-Stitches

Size 11 seed beads and two strands of floss combine to make these unique Beaded Cross-Stitches (fig. 11). Check to make sure your needle will pass through the beads you plan to use.

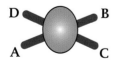

FIG. 11. Come up through the Inchie at A. Pass needle and thread through the seed bead and then go down at B. Come up again at C and pass the needle and thread back through the seed bead in the same direction, with the needle going into the bead on the A side and coming out on the B side. Go down at D and adjust the seed bead so that it sits in the middle of the cross-stitch.

Scatter Stitches

Small straight stitches scattered about randomly fill a space between quilting lines nicely. Use 1–3 strands of floss or try a bit of metallic thread to make Scatter Stitches (fig. 12).

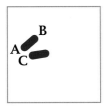

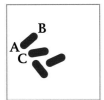

FIG. 12. Come up through the Inchie at A. Go down at B, a short ⅛" away. Come up a short distance away at C and make another short stitch in a random direction. Make as many stitches in varying directions as desired.

Satin Stitches

Satin stitches can add a swath of contrasting color and texture, especially with variegated floss. Use 2–3 strands of floss to make Satin Stitches (fig. 13). Plan to fill an area between quilting lines, or mark lines on the Inchie if desired.

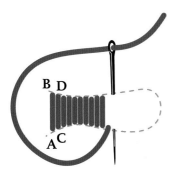

FIG. 13. Come up through the Inchie at A. Go down at B, and come back up at C, right next to point A. Go down at D, right next to point B. Continue in this manner until the area is filled with stitches.

Beribbon It

Many silk ribbon embroidery stitches are not suitable because of the stress on the delicate ribbon as it's pulled through the Inchies. But there are a few that can be used to good effect to add floral accents.

Silk ribbon embroidery should be worked fairly loosely to maintain dimension and a lush effect. Keep the ribbon flat as you form the stitches; if allowed to twist, the ribbon will simply look like a thick thread.

Threading the Needle

Use 12"–16" of ribbon and thread one end through the eye of the needle. Lock the ribbon to the needle's eye (fig. 14).

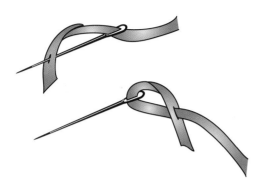

FIG. 14. Pierce the short tail end of the ribbon with the point of the needle about ¼" from the end of the ribbon. Pull the needle through the end of the ribbon. Pull the long end of the ribbon until the short end is about ¼" from the eye of the needle to lock the silk ribbon onto the needle eye.

Knotting the Ribbon

Make a soft knot in the end of the ribbon (fig. 15).

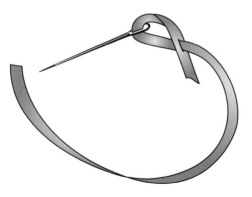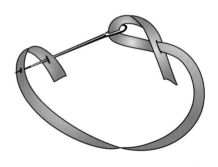

FIG. 15. Hold the needle in one hand and the end of the ribbon in the other. Make a short running stitch in the end of the ribbon with the needle. Pull the needle and ribbon all the way through this running stitch to form a soft knot.

Beginning and Ending Stitches

To keep the knots on the back of the Inchie as flat as possible, take the first stitch through the backing fabric only as shown in figure 2 on page 22, positioning the knot toward the middle.

To end your stitching, take two small stitches through the backing fabric only. Pull tight and trim the ribbon to ⅛".

Colonial Knots

Refer to figure 10 on page 26 and work Colonial Knots in 4mm silk ribbon.

Spider Web Roses

A lush and full Spider Web Rose is the perfect focal point for the center of an Inchie. You'll need a bit of embroidery floss and 4–7mm silk ribbon to make the rose shown in figure 16.

FIG. 16. Using two strands of embroidery floss, form the anchor stitches. Come up at A, go down at B, and come up at C, bringing the needle over the thread as it passes between A and B. Go down at D, forming a Y shape. Add two more equal stitches, one on each side of the Y, forming five spokes. Secure the floss. With silk ribbon, come up in the center of the spokes and begin weaving the ribbon over and under the spokes in a counterclockwise direction. Let the ribbon twist and keep it loose for the best effect. Continue weaving over and under until the spokes are covered.

Ruffle Flowers

Freeform Ruffle Flowers are fun and easy to make. Add seed beads in the center. Use 3" lengths of 4–7mm silk ribbon to make Ruffle Flowers (fig. 17).

FIG. 17. Fold under both short ends of the ribbon and baste along one long edge. Gather up the long edge until a flower is formed, and stitch the two short ends together with a small running stitch. Place in the desired position on the Inchie and tack down. Add seed beads or Colonial Knots in the flower centers.

Leaf Stitches

Leaf Stitches are the perfect accent for flower motifs. Use 4mm silk ribbon to make Leaf Stitches (fig. 18).

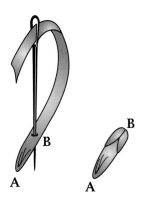

FIG. 18. Come up at A and lay the ribbon flat on the surface of the Inchie. Pierce the ribbon in the middle and go down at B. Pull the ribbon all the way through the Inchie until it curls a bit on either side of B and the ribbon forms a leaf tip. Do not pull tightly or the leaf effect will be lost.

Special Embellishment Techniques: Other Things to Do with Inchies

You'll want to use beading and embroidery stitches on many, if not most, of your Inchies. But don't stop there! There are other special techniques that you may wish to try.

Brads and Eyelets

It's best to place brads close to the center, so that the tails don't show around the edge after they are opened on the back. Use an X-Acto® knife to cut a slit all the way through the Inchie just long enough for the metal tails on the brad to fit. Push the tails through the slit until the brad sits on the surface. Turn it over, open the metal tails, and flatten them against the back. If necessary, you can trim a bit off of the metal tails with a wire cutter, but be sure to leave enough of the tails to keep the brad in place.

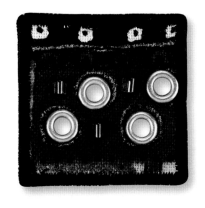

To insert an eyelet, mark the desired location and cut a hole the size of the eyelet with a hole cutter. Insert the eyelet and push it all the way through until it's flush with the surface. Turn the Inchie over and use an eyelet setting tool to flatten the back of the eyelet.

Hot-fix Crystals

Hot-fix crystals come in a wide variety of colors and sizes. They add a lovely sparkle to Inchies.

Use tweezers to place crystals as desired, then hold the hot-fix crystal heat tool on each crystal for eight seconds (a few seconds more for larger crystals) to bond the crystal to the fabric.

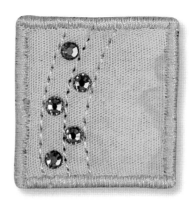

Colored Copper Wire

Copper wire comes in many colors and can be formed into shapes to use as embellishments on Inchies.

Cut copper wire with wire cutters (never with scissors!). Use a wire wrapping jig or round-nosed pliers to make simple shapes and spirals. Attach the wire shape with beading thread and a seed bead using the Seed Spots method (page 23), or tack it in place with coordinating beading thread.

Fusible Ribbon and Trim

Use fusible ribbon and trim either before or after quilting and edge stitching your Inchies. Use a mini iron to fuse the ribbon or trim. Protect it with a non-stick pressing cloth or cover the sole plate of the iron with a bit of self-adhesive Teflon® (see Resources, page 78).

Fibers

Use a needle and beading thread as a loop to guide the fibers through an eyelet in one corner. Tie a lark's head knot or overhand knot to secure.

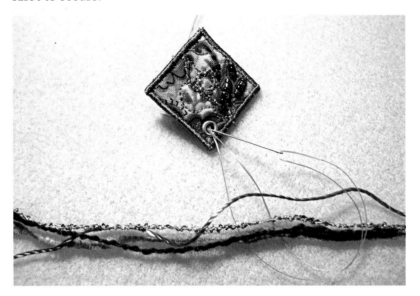

To make a little bird's nest, wrap two or three different fibers together around your finger a couple of times, then slip the loop off and hold it in place on the Inchie. Using beading thread, come up through the fiber nest, pass the needle and thread through a seed bead, and go back down through the Inchie, pulling the thread tight to secure the bead and part of the fiber nest at the same time. Add enough beads around the nest in clusters to attach the fibers securely.

Favorite Quiltmaking Techniques

Fabric Preparation

I recommend prewashing all fabrics to pre-shrink and remove sizing and excess dye. Wash in cold water with a mild soap or detergent, dry in the dryer, and remove promptly to control wrinkles. Fold the fabric neatly with the selvages together so it's ready for rotary cutting.

Make Accuracy a Habit

Use the same ruler throughout a project, as even rulers made by the same manufacturer can vary. Cut the fabrics for your quilt in a well lit area, and use a fresh blade in the rotary cutter. To make accurate templates, lay thin translucent template plastic over the paper pattern and trace the curved lines of the pattern. Mark dots at the corners of straight edges of the template and connect the dots with a ruler for the straightest edge. Transfer all markings to the plastic template and use a mini hole punch or a large needle to make holes where the dots are. Cut out the

Tip! When you trace the template onto the fabric, you're actually adding the width of the drawn line to the dimension of the template. You'll need to cut just inside the drawn line on the fabric so that your patchwork piece is the right size.

template with scissors, cutting on the center of the drawn line.

Turn the templates face down and trace onto the wrong side of the fabric. It's safe to use a Pigma® Micron® pen to trace around templates, since you'll be cutting away the drawn line when you cut out the fabric piece. Transfer dots through the holes to the fabric with a removable marker or chalk pencil. When you cut out the fabric pieces, use small, very sharp scissors and cut just inside the drawn line.

Check your seam allowances to be sure they are an accurate ¼". Small differences can add up to big problems as you piece blocks together and the quilt gets bigger.

Pressing for Success

Press patchwork seams as you go during construction for best results. Use a dry iron on a cotton setting and gently press seam allowances in the direction indicated in the pattern. Don't press too firmly with the iron as this can leave shiny marks on the fabric or cause the seam to open too far. You don't want the sewing thread to show at the seam line. Use steam sparingly, if at all. Save the steam setting on the iron for that last thorough pressing of the quilt top before basting together with batting and backing for quilting.

Satin Stitch Appliqué

Satin stitching is an easy way to anchor fusible appliqué motifs and it adds a dimensional finish around the edge. Use 40wt. rayon, 50wt. or 60wt. cotton, or even #100 silk thread in a color that matches or coordinates well with the appliqué motif on the top. Use 60wt. cotton bobbin thread on the bottom. Choose a Microtex/Sharp machine needle in a size that works with the thread you've chosen.

Set your machine for a narrow, very short zigzag stitch and use an open-toed embroidery presser foot. Place a piece of medium weight tear-away stabilizer behind the fabric and secure with pins if necessary. To begin sewing, center the edge of the appliqué motif under the presser foot and take one stitch, bringing the needle down and back up again, while holding the top thread. Pull up on the top thread to bring the bobbin thread to the top of the quilt, and hold both threads firmly while you begin sewing.

Follow the edge of the appliqué motif with the machine, guiding the fabric through curves and around corners. On corners and sharp curves, stop with the needle down in the fabric on the outside of the curve or corner, lift the presser foot and turn the fabric, then lower the presser foot to continue sewing. When you reach a point in the design where you need to stop sewing, leave the thread tails long enough so that you can pull them to the back of the fabric and tie a knot before trimming, unless you plan to sew over them with another line of satin stitching.

Beautiful Borders

The first step to beautiful quilt borders is measuring the quilt top accurately. To apply straight borders, measure the quilt from top to bottom and cut the side border strips to this length. Pin the borders to the sides of the quilt top and sew. Measure the quilt top from side to side, including the side borders, and cut the top and bottom borders to this length. Pin the borders to the top and bottom of the quilt top and sew. Repeat this process for subsequent borders.

To apply mitered borders, measure the quilt top and add two times the desired width of the borders to this measurement. Add 4" to this measurement as insurance and cut the border strips to this length. Subtract ½" from the quilt top measurement, divide this number in half and make a dot at this Distance A from the center of the border strip on each side as shown in figure 1. Mark a dot on the quilt top on each corner, ¼" from each edge.

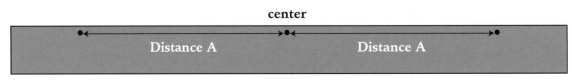

Distance A = (Quilt width – ½") ÷ 2

FIG. 1.

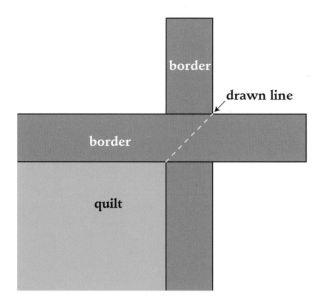

border

drawn line

border

quilt

FIG. 2.

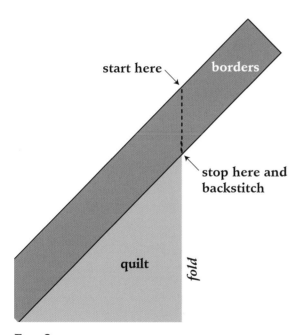

start here **borders**

stop here and backstitch

quilt *fold*

FIG. 3.

RIGHT: INCHIE STAR. Project featured on pages 72–77.

Match the center dot on the border to the center of the quilt edge, and the dots at the ends of the borders to the corner dots on the quilt. Sew the border to the quilt, stopping at the dots and backstitching. Sew all four borders to the quilt in this manner and press seam allowances toward the borders.

To form the miters, lay the quilt top face down on a large gridded cutting mat and work with one corner at a time. Line up the edges of the borders with the grid on the mat, and make sure everything is smooth and flat. Allow the long ends of the borders to overlap at the corner so that they lie flat. Use a ruler to draw a line with a mechanical or chalk pencil from the corner of the quilt top to the point at which the two borders cross (fig. 2).

Fold the quilt diagonally and line up the borders. Pin well and stitch on the marked line, starting at the outside edge of the borders and stitching toward the quilt (fig. 3). Stop stitching and backstitch when you reach the quilt. Open the corner and lay it flat on the cutting table to check that it is square and flat. Trim the seam allowance to ¼" and press to one side. Repeat for each corner of the quilt.

Faced Finishes

A faced edge is a nice alternative to a binding finish and it's easy to do. Trim the batting and backing even with the quilt top. Measure the quilt from top to bottom, subtract 1½", and cut two facing strips to this length for the sides. Measure the quilt from side to side, and cut two facing strips to this length for the top and bottom. Press one long raw edge of each facing strip under ¼".

Pin the unpressed edge of a top facing strip to the top edge of the quilt and sew with a ¼" seam, starting at the lower pressed edge, pivoting at the corner, and sewing across the long edge. Pivot at the next corner, and sew to the pressed edge. Repeat for the bottom facing.

Pin and sew the side facing strips to the quilt, matching raw edges and centering on the side edges, allowing the facing strips to overlap the top and bottom strips. Trim the corners of the quilt *batting and backing only* to a scant ⅛" from the stitching to remove some of the bulk from the corners. Gently press the facing strips away from the quilt center. Turn the entire facing to the back of the quilt, carefully pushing out the corners. Press the facings to the back with the iron, tucking the raw edges of the side facing the strips under the top and bottom facings at the edges. Slip stitch the folded edges to the back of the quilt to finish.

LEFT: INCHIE SAMPLER, with faced edges. Project featured on pages 38–40.

Quilt Patterns

Colorwash Inchie Quilting Designs

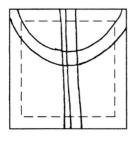 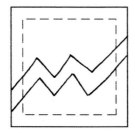 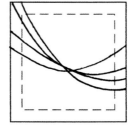 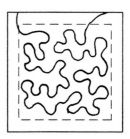

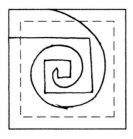 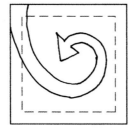 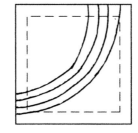 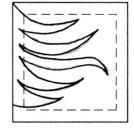

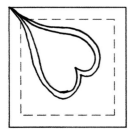 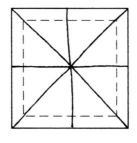 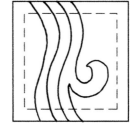 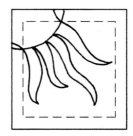

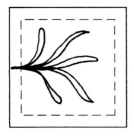 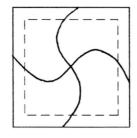 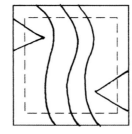 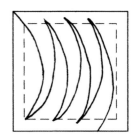

  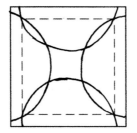 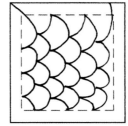

INCHIE SAMPLER

DIMINUTIVE DETAILS

Luxury yarns or fibers add loads of textural interest to this quilt. Couch fibers onto the Inchies during the quilting process, or hang them from the Inchies after other embellishments are finished, using eyelets at the bottom corners.

INCHIE SAMPLER

Make this fun sampler quilt to get acquainted with most of the construction and embellishment techniques presented in the book.

Quilt Size: 12" x 12"

Materials

40" wide fabric

- 1 yard ombre fabric for background, Inchies, Inchie backing, quilt backing, and facing
- ¼ yard print fabric for Inchies and Inchie backing
- Batting at least 14" x 14"
- Filler for Inchies at least 5" x 6¾"
- Stiffener 5½" x 7¾"
- Beads, fibers, eyelets, and other embellishments as desired
- ¼ yard Velcro® brand Fabric Fusion tape
- Fabric glue

Cutting

From the ombre background fabric, cut:

- ➡ One 14" x 14" square for quilt backing
- ➡ One 1¼" strip; subcut into six 1¼" x 2½" rectangles. Cut these rectangles from the entire width of the fabric strip so that you have a range of values as shown in figure 1.
- ➡ Two 1½" strips for facing
- ➡ One 6½" strip; from this strip, cut:
- ○ One 5¾" x 5⅜" rectangle for piece A
- ○ One 5¾" x 5" rectangle for piece B
- ○ One 5¾" x 3⅛" rectangle for piece C
- ○ One 3⅞" x 6½" rectangle for piece D
- ○ One 3⅞" x 6½" rectangle for piece E
- ○ One 7¼" x 6½" rectangle for piece F

> **Tip!** Use figure 2 on page 40 as a guide when cutting the ombre fabric pieces. Pay special attention to the shading direction of each piece when cutting and sewing to get the desired effect, with the arrows pointing to the light side of each section.

From the backing fabric, cut:

- ➡ One 4" x 5" rectangle for Inchie backing

From the print fabric, cut:

- ➡ One 3" x 4" rectangle for Inchies
- ➡ One 6" x 4¾" rectangle for Inchie backing

From the filler, cut:

- ➡ One 5" x 3¾" rectangle
- ➡ One 4" x 3" rectangle

From the stiffener, cut:

- ➡ One 5½" x 4¼" rectangle
- ➡ One 4½" x 3½" rectangle

FIG. 1.

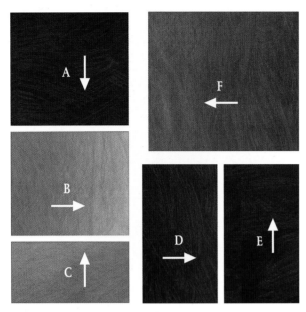

FIG. 2.

FIG. 3.

FIG. 4.

Make the Quilt

Join the pieces as shown, positioning the fabrics so the arrows point toward the lightest side of each piece.

Quilt and finish

Layer the quilt with batting and backing. Quilt as desired.

Finish the quilt edges with a facing using the 1½" strips as described on page 36.

Make the Inchies

Make a sandwich with the 3" x 4" print fabric rectangle, the 3" x 4" filler rectangle, 4½" x 3½" stiffener rectangle, and the 4" x 5" ombre fabric rectangle (fig. 3). Make a second sandwich with the 1¼" x 2½" pieces of the ombre fabric arranged as shown (fig. 4), the 5" x 3¾" filler rectangle, the 5½" x 4¼" stiffener rectangle, and the 6" x 4¾" print fabric rectangle.

Refer to the Basic Inchie Instructions (pages 12–20) to make 24 Inchies, 12 from each of the Inchie fabrics. Embellish with beads, wire, decorative threads, crystals, or found objects as desired. Use eyelets on two of the Inchies, and attach hanging fibers. Refer to Making Them Stick (page 17) to attach the Inchies with Velcro on pieces B and F. Use fabric glue to attach the Inchies to pieces A, C, and D, and attach the Inchies on piece E with beading links. Position the Inchies on each section of the quilt as shown in the photo, or arrange them as desired.

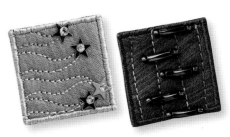

INCHIE ART GALLERY

This quilt design is great for a collection of Inchies from one fabric or Inchies collected from quilting friends in a swap!

INCHIE ART GALLERY

Quilt Size: 13¼" x 17"

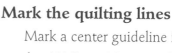

Materials

40" wide fabric

- 1 yard blue fabric for background, Inchie backing, and facing
- ⅛ yard for Inchies
- ¾ yard for backing
- Batting at least 18" x 21"
- 7" x 9" filler for Inchies
- 7½" x 9½" stiffener
- Beads, fibers, and other embellishments as desired
- 1⅛ yards Velcro® brand Fabric Fusion tape

Cutting

From the background fabric, cut:

➡ Two 1½" strips for facing
➡ One 21" strip; from this strip, cut:
- One 18" x 21" rectangle for quilt backing
- One 13¾" x 17½" rectangle for quilt top
➡ One 8" x 10" rectangle for Inchie backing

From the Inchie fabric, cut:

➡ One 7" x 9" rectangle

Make the Quilt
Mark the quilting lines

Mark a center guideline from top to bottom on the 13¼" x 17" rectangle. Measure 1⅜" to the right of the center guideline and mark the first quilting line from top to bottom. Mark two more lines to the right of the first quilting line in the same manner. Repeat for the left side.

Mark a center guideline across the rectangle from side to side. Measure up 2¼" from this center guideline, and mark a quilting line. Measure up 1⅜" from this line and mark the next quilting line. Mark two more lines above the second quilting line in the same manner, marking each line 1⅜" from the preceding line. Repeat for the bottom.

Tip! Choose an Inchie fabric with a variety of different motifs and colors, and then divide the Inchies into groups of similar design after they are cut. Add embellishments to enhance the subtle differences in the groups. Viewers might be surprised that all the Inchies were made from just one fabric!

Quilt and Finish

Layer the quilt with batting and backing.

Quilt on the marked quilting lines, quilting all lines from top to bottom first, and then side to side.

Finish the quilt edges with a facing using the 1½" strips as described on page 36.

Tip! Use a variegated thread that contrasts nicely with the background fabric and complements the colors of the Inchie fabric to quilt the background quilt.

Make the Inchies

Layer the Inchie fabric with the filler, stiffener, and backing to make the Inchie sandwich. Refer to the Basic Inchie Instructions Section (pages 12–20) to make 48 Inchies.

Embellish the Inchies with beads, wire, decorative threads, crystals, or found objects as desired. Refer to Making Them Stick (page 17) to attach the Inchies with Velcro, positioning them as shown in the diagram, arranging the Inchies as desired.

DIMINUTIVE DETAILS

A few of the Inchies on this quilt were not embellished with beads or embroidery, since the design of the fabric, quilting, and couched threads was quite beautiful as it was. Don't be afraid to let an Inchie stand on its own without further embellishment if the design of the fabric and couched trims is interesting enough.

INCHIE PETIT FOURS

These Inchie Petit Fours look good enough to eat, with silk ribbon roses, bows, buttons, and beads. Yum!

INCHIE PETIT FOURS

Quilt Size: 12¾" x 12¾"

Materials
40 " wide fabric

- ⅛ yard brown fabric for squares
- ¼ yard cream fabric for squares and Inchie backing
- ¼ yard print fabric for Inchies
- ⅛ yard pink fabric for inner border
- ¼ yard fabric for outer border
- 1 fat quarter plaid fabric for bias binding
- ½ yard fabric for backing
- Batting at least 14" x 14"
- 5½" x 5½" filler for Inchies
- 6" x 6" stiffener
- Beads, tiny buttons, silk ribbons, and other embellishments as desired
- Fabric glue

Tip! Don't like Petit Fours? Choose any medium to large multicolor print you like, and then choose light and dark background fabrics to make the quilt. Choose quilting designs and embellishments to accent your theme.

Cutting

From the brown fabric, cut:
- ➡ One 1½" strip, subcut into thirteen 1½" squares

From the cream fabric, cut:
- ➡ One 1½" strip, subcut into twelve 1½" squares
- ➡ One 6½" square for Inchie backing

From the inner border fabric, cut:
- ➡ One ¾" strip

From the outer border fabric, cut:
- ➡ Two 3" strips

From the binding fabric, cut:
- ➡ One 14" square, cut into bias strips

From the Inchie fabric, cut:
- ➡ One 5½" x 5½" square

Make the Quilt
Lay out the block

Lay out the brown and cream 1½" squares in a checkerboard arrangement (fig. 1).

Sew the squares together into rows, then join the rows, pressing seam allowances toward the brown fabric.

FIG. 1.

Tip! For a more three-dimensional look, add piping to the edges of the block instead of a flange.

DIMINUTIVE DETAILS

If desired, choose one Inchie and mark the back with a "bite" shape before embellishing. Carefully cut out the bite shape, edge stitch the raw edge, and embellish as desired. Glue this Inchie to the outer border.

Add the borders

Measure the quilt top and cut four strips to this length from the inner border fabric.

Fold the strips in half lengthwise, and sew to the edges of the quilt top, first the sides and then the top and bottom, to create the flanged ⅛" inner border. Attach the outer borders and miter the corners.

Quilt and finish

Use the border quilting designs provided to mark the border, if desired (fig. 1).

Layer the quilt with batting and backing.

Quilt three or four "clamshells" on the sides of each square to resemble paper cups. Stitch in the ditch between the borders, and quilt the outer border designs.

Use your favorite binding method to bind the quilt with the 2¼" strips of the plaid fabric.

Make the Inchies

Layer the Inchie fabric with the filler, stiffener, and backing. Refer to the Basic Inchie Instructions (pages 12–20) to make 25 Inchies.

Embellish the Inchies with beads, embroidery floss, decorative threads, silk ribbon, small buttons or charms, or other objects as desired. Refer to the instructions for Basic Silk Ribbon Embroidery (pages 27–30) and Basic Embroidery Stitches (pages 25–27), and consult the Resources section (page 78) for other embroidery and silk ribbon embroidery reference books. Refer to Making Them Stick (page 17) to attach the Inchies with fabric glue, one in each square.

Life is like a box of Petit Fours

DIMINUTIVE DETAILS

Inchies make a fun fringe! Attach Inchies to the very bottom edge of the quilt with beads, right at the edge of and through the binding. Use one, two, or even three Inchies, depending on the desired look and how many Inchies are left after making Inchie chains for the quilt surface.

INCHIE PORTRAITS

Start with a pre-printed fabric panel, photos transferred to fabric, orphaned blocks, or machine embroidery motifs to make a custom-sized quilt with coordinating Inchie accents.

INCHIE PORTRAITS

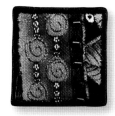

Quilt Size: 12" x 33" *(approximate)*

Materials

40" wide fabric

○ Three portraits, approximately 6" x 8", but not larger than 6" x 9"
○ 1 yard background fabric
○ ¼ yard print fabric for Inchies
○ ¼ yard for binding
○ ½ yard fabric for backing
○ Batting at least 14" x 36"
○ 6" x 7" filler for Inchies
○ 6½" x 7½" stiffener
○ Beads, fibers, wire, found objects, and other embellishments as desired

Cutting

From the background fabric, cut:
➡ Two 5" strips
➡ One 3¼" strip
➡ One 3" strip
➡ One 2" strip
➡ One 7" x 8" rectangle for Inchie backing

From the binding fabric, cut:
➡ Two 2¼" strips

From the backing fabric, cut:
➡ One 14" x 36" rectangle

From the Inchie fabric, cut:
➡ One 6" x 7" rectangle

Make the Quilt
Arrange the portraits

Trim the portraits to the desired size, leaving a ¼" seam allowance all the way around.

Cut two segments from the 5" strips a bit longer than the top portrait and sew one strip to each side, centering the portrait on the strip. Press seam allowances toward the background strips (fig. 1).

Repeat this using 3¼" strips for the middle portraits and 5" strips for the bottom portrait.

Trim the strips even with the top and bottom of each portrait.

Add separator strips and borders

Arrange the top and bottom portraits so that they are off center, with a bit more space on one side for the Inchies to hang (fig. 2).

Cut the 2" and 3" strips in half and place them as shown.

FIG. 1.

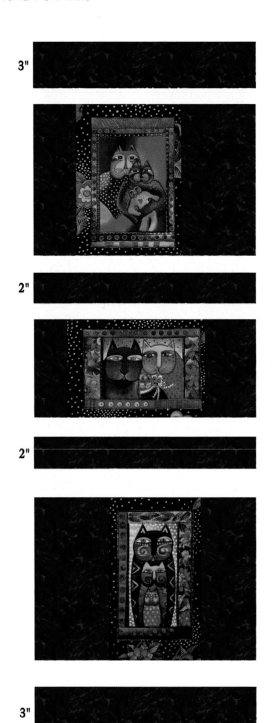

3"

2"

2"

3"

FIG. 2.

Tip! Don't worry if your portraits are oddly sized or not all the same size. It's actually more interesting! This quilt is sized "on the fly" as it's constructed. So it doesn't really matter what size the portraits are.

Sew the quilt

Sew the quilt top together in rows as shown. Begin at the top, and flip the top border over onto the top portrait row; pin together and sew.

Repeat for the remaining rows, lining up the portraits and separator strips as desired as you sew. Press the seam allowance toward the borders and separator strips.

Use a ruler and rotary cutter to trim the side edges of the quilt so they are straight and the top and bottom corners are square.

Quilt and finish

Layer the quilt with batting and backing. Quilt as desired. Use your favorite binding method to bind the quilt with the 2¼" strips of the binding fabric.

Make the Inchies

Refer to the Basic Inchie Instructions (pages 12–20) to make about 30 Inchies. The number needed will vary, depending on the finished size of your quilt.

Embellish the Inchies with beads, decorative threads, brads, crystals, or found objects as desired. Refer to Making Them Stick (page 17) and use beads to attach the Inchies to the quilt, positioning Inchies on the quilt as shown or arranging them as desired.

INCHIE HOUSE PARTY

Inchies were born to be swapped! Quilting friends can organize an Inchie House Party and swap Inchies to display as the windows of the house.

INCHIE HOUSE PARTY

Quilt Size: 18¼" x 26½"

Finished Block Size: 18" x 20"

Materials

40 " wide fabric

- ○ ¾ yard blue fabric for background
- ○ ¼ yard each of three green fabrics for hills
- ○ ⅛ yard each or scraps of various fabrics for appliqué shapes
- ○ ¼ yard for outer border
- ○ ½ yard for inner border, binding, and Inchie backing
- ○ Scraps of 12 different fabrics for Inchies
- ○ ¾ yard for backing
- ○ Batting at least 25" x 30"
- ○ 1 yard fusible web
- ○ 1 yard tear-away stabilizer
- ○ 4½" x 6" filler for Inchies
- ○ 5" x 6½" stiffener
- ○ Beads and other embellishments as desired
- ○ ¼ yard Velcro® brand Fabric Fusion tape

FIG. 1.

Cutting

From the blue background fabric, cut:

➡ One 19" x 21" rectangle (piece A)

From the inner border, binding and Inchie backing fabric, cut:

➡ One 1" strip
➡ Three 2¼" strips for binding
➡ One 5½" x 7" rectangle for Inchie backing

From the outer border fabric, cut:

➡ One 3" strip

From the backing fabric, cut:

➡ One 25" x 30" rectangle

From each of the Inchie fabrics, cut:

➡ One 1½" square

Make the Quilt
Make the appliqué block

Make 2 copies of the appliqué design (page 55) at 250%—one to use as a placement diagram and one in reverse for tracing your templates. Trace the reversed pieces B through O onto the paper side of fusible web. Be sure to add a ¼" seam allowance to the outside edges of pieces C, J, L, and M. Roughly cut each fusible web piece out, leaving ¼" outside the drawn line. Fuse lightly to the wrong side of the appliqué fabrics. Cut out the appliqué pieces on the lines.

Trace the Inchie House Party letters (fig. 1) onto piece O with a Pigma Micron pen or other permanent fabric marker before fusing.

Place a Teflon pressing sheet over the enlarged placement diagram. Remove the paper backing from the appliqué pieces and position them in letter order, from B through O. Lightly fuse the pieces together on the Teflon sheet.

When completely cool, remove the fused appliqué pieces as a unit and position on the background. Fuse in place following manufacturer's instructions.

Satin stitch the appliqué block

Refer to the Satin Stitch Appliqué instructions (page 34) to satin stitch each piece to the background fabric, working in the same order as the pieces were fused, from B through O.

Remove the stabilizer from behind each piece before satin stitching the next piece.

Square up and trim the appliqué block to 18½"x 20½".

Add the borders

Attach the inner borders to the top and bottom of the quilt only using the 1" inner border strips (fig. 2). Press seam allowances toward the borders.

Attach the outer borders on the top and bottom of the quilt only using the 3" outer border strips. Press seam allowances toward the borders.

FIG. 2.

FIG. 3.

Quilt and finish

Layer the quilt with batting and backing.

Quilt "in the ditch" just at the outside edge of the satin stitching around each piece. Add other quilted details as desired.

Use your favorite binding method to bind the quilt with the 2¼" strips of the binding fabric.

Make the Inchies

Arrange the Inchie fabrics on the filler, stiffener, and backing (fig. 3). Refer to the Basic Inchie Instructions (pages 12–20) to make 12 Inchies, one from each of the Inchie fabrics. Embellish the Inchies with beads, wire, decorative threads, crystals, or found objects as desired. Refer to Making Them Stick (page 17) to attach the Inchies to the quilt with Velcro, positioning Inchies on the quilt as shown in the photo.

DIMINUTIVE DETAILS

Coordinate an Inchie House Party! Decide on a theme for the Inchies and provide the basic materials, like beading thread, needles, and perhaps some seed beads in colors that fit with the theme. Ask quilting friends to bring other embellishments and arrive with Inchies sewn and ready to embellish. Enjoy a fun afternoon embellishing Inchies together, and then swap so that everyone has a wide variety of Inchies for their own quilt!

Enlarge pattern 250% before tracing. Make 2 copies—one to use as a placement guide and one in reverse for tracing your templates.

PICTURE PERFECT INCHIES

Keeping the Inchies in order as they are cut keeps the design of the Inchie fabric at center stage .

PICTURE PERFECT INCHIES

Quilt Size: 11¼" x 14¼"

Materials

40" wide fabric

- ○ ½ yard background fabric
- ○ ¼ yard Inchie fabric
- ○ ¼ yard inner border fabric
- ○ ½ yard for binding
- ○ ½ yard for backing
- ○ Batting at least 14" x 18"
- ○ 5" x 7" filler for Inchies
- ○ 5½" x 7½" stiffener
- ○ Beads, brads, fibers, and other embellishments as desired
- ○ Fabric glue

Cutting

From the background fabric, cut:
- ➡ Two 2½" strips for outer borders
- ➡ One 7¾" x 9¾" rectangle for quilt center
- ➡ One 6" x 8" rectangle for Inchie backing

From the Inchie fabric, cut:
- ➡ One 5" x 7" rectangle, centering a large design motif in the rectangle

From the inner border fabric, cut:
- ➡ Two ¾" strips; subcut these strips into two 9¾" x ¾" rectangles and two 7¾" x ¾" rectangles

From the binding fabric, cut:
- ➡ Two 1⅝" strips

From the backing fabric, cut:
- ➡ One 14" x 18" rectangle

Make the Quilt
Add the borders

Fold the inner border strips in half lengthwise and sew to the edges of the quilt top matching raw edges, first the sides and then the top and bottom, to make the flanged ⅛" inner border as shown (fig. 1).

Attach the outer borders using the 2½" outer border strips.

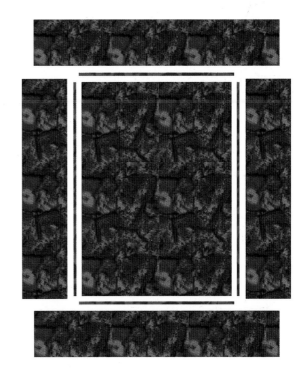

FIG. 1.

Tip! Look for an Inchie fabric that has a large, obvious motif, and select embellishments in colors to accent the colors of the fabric.

Quilt and finish

Mark a grid in the center of the quilt and a design that complements the Inchies in the outer border.

Layer the quilt with batting and backing.

Quilt as desired.

Use your favorite binding method to bind the quilt with the 1⅝" strips of the binding fabric.

Make the Inchies

Layer the Inchie fabric with the filler, stiffener, and backing. Refer to the Basic Inchie Instructions (pages 12–20) to make 24 Inchies. When you cut the Inchies apart, keep them in order so that the picture is still visible. Using permanent marker label each Inchie on the back with a number and an arrow indicating the top.

Embellish the Inchies with beads, decorative threads, crystals, or found objects as desired. Refer to Making Them Stick (page 17) to attach the Inchies with fabric glue, arranging the Inchies in order by the numbers on the back.

DIMINUTIVE DETAILS

The embellisments for these Inchies were carefully chosen to blend well with the fabric motif and colors. Beads and other embellishments were used to add depth and texture to the fabric print, not obscure it, so that the original picture is clear. The embellishments in the background areas should blend in so as not to detract from the main motif. For true luxury and the ultimate sparkle, look for Swarovski® crystal beads in the round number 2 size—hard to find and costly, but worth it.

SHADOW BOX INCHIES

*Easy strip piecing and subtle fabric choices create a "shadow box"
background for Inchies from two or more different fabrics.*

Shadow Box Inchies

Quilt Size: 14½" x 16½"

Materials

40" wide fabric

- ¼ yard light aqua fabric
- ¼ yard blue fabric
- ½ yard purple fabric for outer border and Inchie backing
- ¼ yard turquoise fabric for binding
- ⅛ yard each or scraps of two different fabrics for Inchies
- ¾ yard for backing
- Batting at least 18" x 20"
- 5" x 6¼" filler for Inchies
- 5½" x 6¾" stiffener
- Beads, brads, fibers, and other embellishments as desired
- ½ yard Velcro® brand Fabric Fusion tape

Cutting

From the aqua, cut:
- ➡ Three 1½" strips for blocks, separator strips, and inner borders

From the blue, cut:
- ➡ Two 1½" strips for blocks, separator strips, and inner borders

From the purple fabric, cut:
- ➡ Two 2¾" strips for outer borders
- ➡ One 6" x 7¼" rectangle for Inchie backing

From the turquoise fabric, cut:
- ➡ Two 1⅝" strips for binding

From the backing fabric, cut:
- ➡ One 18" x 20" rectangle

From each of the Inchie fabrics, cut:
- ➡ One 2½" x 6¼" rectangle

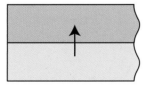

Fig. 1.

Make the Quilt

Make the strip-set

Sew one 1½" aqua strip lengthwise to one 1½" blue strip (fig. 1). Press the seam allowance toward the darker strip. Cut into four sections, approximately 10" long each.

Tip! Create a color story and let your fabric choices be inspired by embellishment colors, styles, or materials that you plan to use on the Inchies. Choose quilting designs to accent the theme.

Sew the sections together (fig. 2) to make one strip-set with eight strips. Press seam allowances toward the darker strips.

Cross cut the strip-set into five 1½" segments.

Assemble the quilt

Measure the completed strip-set segments and cut five separator strips to this length from the 1½" aqua strips.

Arrange the strip-set segments and the aqua separator strips as shown (fig. 3).

Sew the strips together, and press seam allowances toward the separator strips.

Attach the inner borders to the quilt in order beginning with border 1 (fig. 3). Cut the strips for borders 1 and 2 from the 1½" aqua strips, and the strips for borders 3 and 4 from the 1½" blue strips.

Attach the outer borders to the quilt, first the side borders and then the top and bottom, using the outer border strips.

Quilt and finish

Layer the quilt with batting and backing.

Quilt as desired.

Use your favorite binding method to bind the quilt with the 1⅝" strips of the binding fabric.

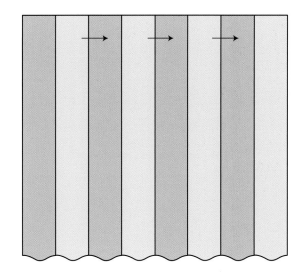

FIG. 2.

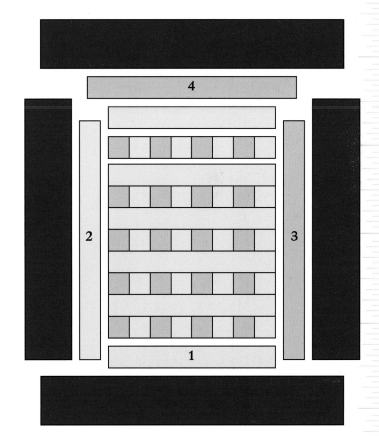

FIG. 3.

Fig. 4.

Make the Inchies

Arrange the Inchie fabrics on the filler, stiffener, and backing (fig. 4).

Refer to the Basic Inchie Instructions (pages 12–20) to make 20 Inchies, ten from each of the Inchie fabrics. Embellish the Inchies with beads, wire, decorative threads, crystals, or found objects as desired. Refer to Making Them Stick (page 17) to attach the Inchies with Velcro, positioning Inchies on the quilt as shown in the quilt photo, arranging the Inchies as desired.

DIMINUTIVE DETAILS

You may have noticed that this quilt has one special Inchie as it appears on the cover. It's easy to add an Inchie of a different color or fabric to your quilt since the Inchies are removable! You may have an extra from another quilt or Inchie fabric experiment just lying about, but if not, make a "mini" Inchie sandwich for just one Inchie. Fasten the extra Inchie to the back of the quilt with Velcro.

INCHIE CHESS

Inchies are perfect as game pieces! Print, trace, or machine embroider "pieces" and embellish with beads and trims fit for royalty.

INCHIE CHESS

Quilt Size: 18½" x 18½"

Materials

40" wide fabric

○ ⅛ yard dark print
○ ⅛ yard medium print
○ ½ yard light beige fabric for Inchies, Inchie backing, and first inner border
○ ¼ yard brown fabric for second inner border
○ ¼ yard black fabric for outer border
○ ¾ yard dark brown fabric for binding and backing
○ ½ yard for backing
○ Batting at least 22" x 22"
○ 6" x 10½" filler for Inchies
○ 6½" x 11½" stiffener
○ Beads, fibers, and other embellishments as desired
○ Bubble Jet Set 2000® ink set and Bubble Jet Rinse (for printed Inchies only)
○ Fabric glue

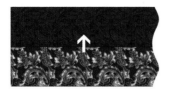

FIG. 1.

Cutting

From the dark print, cut:
➡ Two 2" strips

From the medium print, cut:
➡ Two 2" strips

From the light beige fabric, cut:
➡ Two ¾" strips for first inner border
➡ One 9" x 11½" rectangle (for printed or traced Inchies only)
➡ Two 6¼" x 7" rectangles for Inchie backing

From the brown fabric, cut:
➡ Two 1" strips for second inner border

From the black fabric, cut:
➡ Two 2½" strips for outer borders

From dark brown fabric, cut:
➡ Three 2¼" strips for binding

From the backing fabric, cut:
➡ One 22" square

Make the Quilt
Make the strip-set

Sew one 2" dark print strip lengthwise to one 2" medium print strip (fig. 1). Press the seam allowance toward the darker strip. Make two strip-sets. Cut each strip-set in half crosswise for a total of four sections, approximately 20" each.

Sew the sections together to make one strip-set with eight strips (fig. 2). Press the seam allowances toward the darker strips.

Cross cut the strip-set into eight 2" segments.

Assemble the quilt

Arrange the segments in rows, alternating the direction of the rows for a checkerboard arrangement (fig. 3).

Sew the rows together, matching seams, and press all the seam allowances in the same direction.

For each side of the quilt, sew the border strips together into one unit as shown and press the seam allowances toward the outer borders.

Attach the borders as a unit to each side of the quilt and miter the corners as described on pages 34–35, matching the seams between the borders at the corners.

Quilt and finish

Layer the quilt with batting and backing.

Quilt as desired.

Use your favorite binding method to bind the quilt with the 2¼" strips of the dark brown fabric.

Make the Inchies

Transfer the chess piece graphics to the fabric. Iron the 9" x 11½" rectangle of light beige fabric to the shiny side of freezer paper and trim to 8½" x 11". Scan the chess piece graphics or download the graphics in a ready-to-print Adobe PDF file from **www.inchiequilts.com/downloads/chess.pdf.** Print the graphics on the fabric using an ink jet printer and Bubble Jet Set 2000 and Bubble Jet Rinse, following the manufacturer's instructions. You can also use a light box to trace the graphics onto the Inchie fabric.

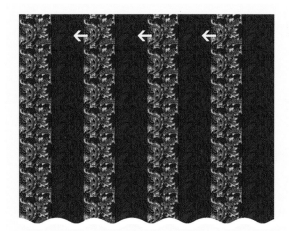

FIG. 2.

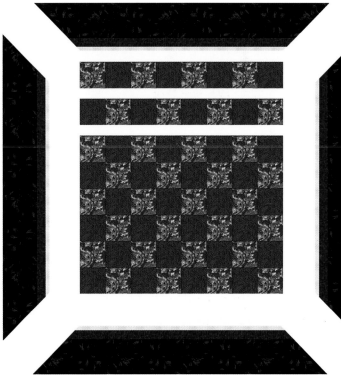

FIG. 3.

Tip! To machine embroider the chess piece Inchies as shown in the quilt photo, visit: www.sanfranciscostitchco.com/inchiechesspiece.html to download the designs. Follow the instructions in the download file to embroider the pieces.

FIG. 4.

DIMINUTIVE DETAILS

Gold and silver beads are embellishments fit for the game of kings. The arrangement of the chess pieces on this quilt is a chess opening called Four Knights, Pillsbury variation. Consult a chess player's handbook if you'd like to arrange the pieces in a different opening in your quilt.

Cut the Inchie fabric in half to separate the light and dark chess pieces. Make two Inchie sandwiches with the printed chess piece fabrics on the filler, stiffener, and backing (fig. 4).

Refer to the Basic Inchie Instructions (page 12–20) to make 32 chess piece Inchies. Embellish the Inchies with beads, decorative threads, crystals, or found objects as desired. Refer to Making Them Stick (page 17) to attach the Inchies with fabric glue, positioning Inchies as shown in the quilt photo.

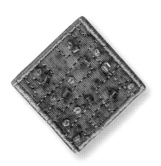

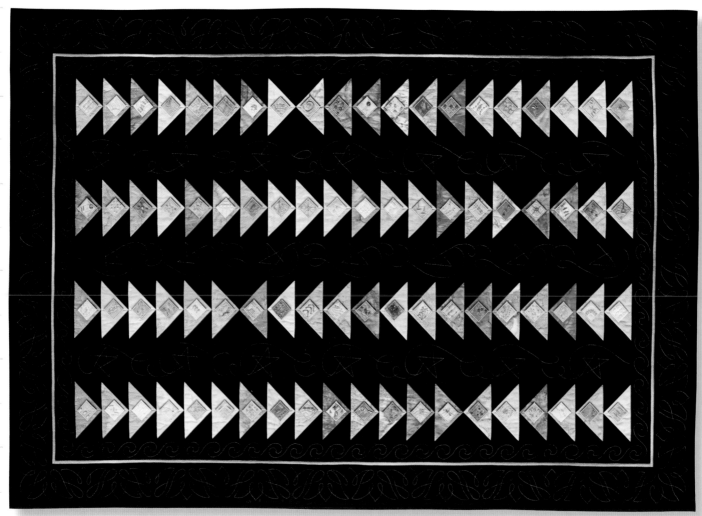

FLYING INCHIES

The traditional Flying Geese block is updated with rainbow colors and the Inchies are attached with Velcro for the ultimate color play quilt.

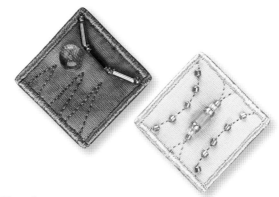

FLYING INCHIES

Quilt Size: 48½" x 33½"

Finished Block Size: 2" x 4"

Materials

40" wide fabric

- ○ 2 yards black fabric for background, Inchie backing, and binding
- ○ ¼ yard ombre fabric for inner border
- ○ One fat eighth yard each of 20 different fabrics for Flying Geese and Inchies
- ○ 1¾ yard for backing
- ○ Batting at least 53" x 38"
- ○ Filler for Inchies at least 5" x 25"
- ○ Stiffener at least 5½" x 27½"
- ○ Beads and other embellishments as desired
- ○ 1¾ yards Velcro® brand Fabric Fusion tape

> **Tip!** Plan to use the Easy Star & Geese ruler for this project for fast and accurate Flying Geese (see Resources, page 78). Then choose a mini jelly roll with 20 different 2½" strips for the Flying Geese blocks and Inchies. Jelly roll strips are color coordinated and precut to just the right size for a super quick start!

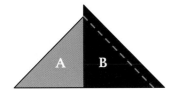

Fig. 1.

Cutting

From each of the Flying Geese fabrics, cut:
- ➡ One 2½" square for Inchies
- ➡ One 5¼" x 5¼" square twice on the diagonal to yield four center triangles

From the background fabric, cut:
- ➡ Four 3" strips for the outer border
- ➡ Five 2¼" strips for binding
- ➡ Two 3½" separator strips
- ➡ Four 2" strips
- ➡ One 6" strip, subcut into five 6" squares for Inchie backing
- ➡ Seven 2⅞" strips, subcut into eighty 2⅞" squares. Cut each square once on the diagonal to make two triangles.

From the inner border fabric, cut:
- ➡ Four ¾" strips

From the backing fabric, cut:
- ➡ One 38" x 53" rectangle

From the filler, cut:
- ➡ Five 5" squares

From the stiffener, cut:
- ➡ Five 5½" squares

Make the Quilt
Make the Flying Geese blocks

Sew a side triangle B to each middle triangle A. Match one pointed end of triangle B to the pointed end of triangle A (fig. 1). The other pointed end of triangle B will extend beyond the

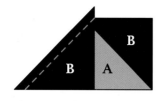

FIG. 2.

FIG. 3.

FIG. 4.

end of triangle A as shown. Press the seam allowance toward triangle B. Trim the excess point of triangle B even with the edge of triangle A.

Sew a second triangle B to the other side of each triangle A (fig. 2). Press the seam allowance toward triangle B.

Arrange the Flying Geese blocks

Arrange the Flying Geese blocks in four strips of 20 blocks each.

Sew the blocks together and press the seam allowances toward the wide end of each "goose." Where two goose points meet in the middle of the strip, press the seam allowances open (fig. 3).

Assemble the quilt

Measure the Flying Geese strips and cut the 3½" background fabric strips and two of the 2" background fabric strips to this length.

Arrange the Flying Geese strips and the background fabric strips (fig. 4) and sew them together. Press the seam allowances toward the background strips.

Sew the 2" background fabric strips to the top and bottom of the quilt as shown.

Measure the quilt top from top to bottom and cut the two remaining 2" background strips to this length. Sew the strips to the sides of the quilt, and press the seam allowances toward the strips.

Attach the inner and outer borders to the quilt, attaching the top and bottom borders first, then the side borders.

Quilt and finish

Layer the quilt with batting and backing.

Quilt as desired.

Use your favorite binding method to bind the quilt with the 2¼" strips of the background fabric.

Make the Inchies

Arrange four of the 2½" Inchie fabric squares on the filler, stiffener, and backing as shown (fig. 5). Make five Inchie sandwiches, with four Inchie fabrics of similar colors together on each sandwich.

Refer to the Basic Inchie Instructions (pages 12–20) to make 80 colorwash Inchies, four from each of the Inchie fabrics. Embellish the Inchies with beads, wire, decorative threads, crystals, or found objects as desired. Refer to Making Them Stick (page 17) to attach the Inchies with Velcro, positioning them on the Flying Geese blocks as shown in the quilt photo. Mix up and arrange the colors as desired.

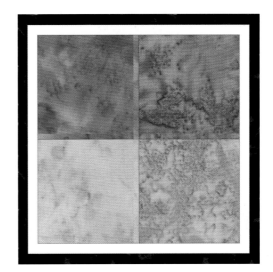

FIG. 5.

DIMINUTIVE DETAILS

When you arrange the Inchies on the quilt, shift the colors and mix them up a bit so that some of the Inchies are more obvious than others. Have fun with your color play and rearrange at will!

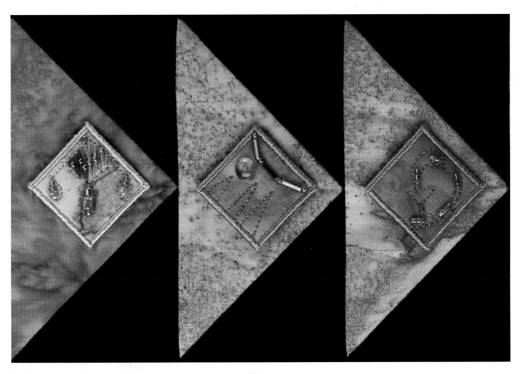

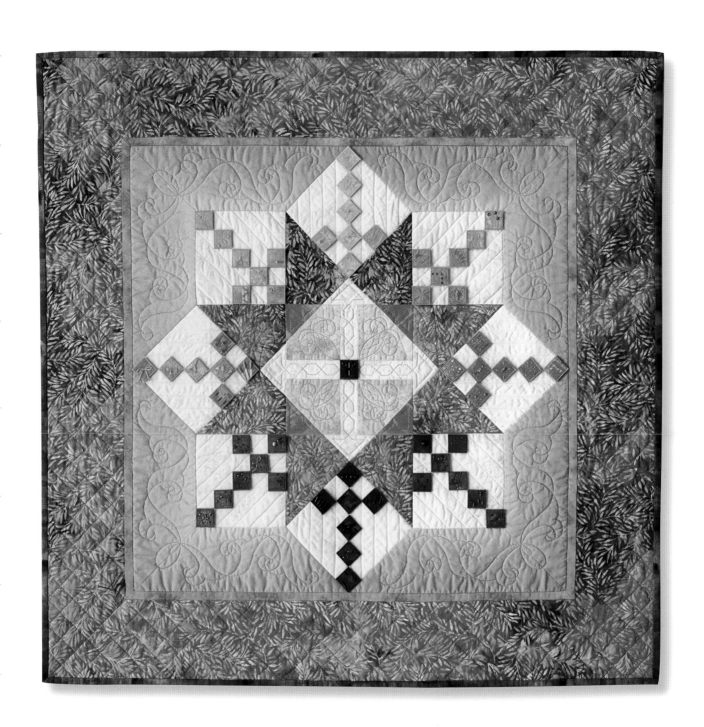

INCHIE STAR

This eight-pointed star is bursting with colorful Inchies. Accurate cutting and piecing make easy work of a complex-looking quilt.

INCHIE STAR

Quilt Size: 34" x 34"
Center block: 24¾" x 24¾"

Materials

40" wide fabric

- 1¼ yards print fabric for outer borders and star points
- ¾ yard light peach fabric for background
- ⅛ yard medium pink fabric for center kites
- ⅛ yard dark pink fabric for center triangles
- ⅛ yard orange fabric for inner border
- ¼ yard purple fabric for binding
- 1¾–3¼ yards ombre fabric for setting pieces*
- ⅛ yard each or scraps of sixteen different fabrics for Inchies
- 1¼ yards for backing
- Batting at least 38" x 38"
- Filler for Inchies at least 5" x 20"
- Stiffener at least 5½" x 22"
- Beads and other embellishments as desired
- 1½ yards Velcro® brand Fabric Fusion tape

*If there is only one complete ombre repeat across the width of the fabric, buy the larger amount of yardage.

Cutting

From the print fabric, cut:
- ➡ Four 4½" strips from the lengthwise grain for outer borders
- ➡ Eight of template A

From the light peach background fabric, cut:
- ➡ One 6" strip, subcut into four 6" squares for Inchie backing
- ➡ Eight of template B
- ➡ Four of template C
- ➡ Four of template E

From the medium pink fabric, cut:
- ➡ Four of template D

From the dark pink fabric, cut:
- ➡ Four of template C
- ➡ One of template F

From the ombre fabric, cut:
- ➡ Four of template G

From the inner border fabric, cut:
- ➡ Four 1" strips

From the binding fabric, cut:
- ➡ Four 2½" strips

From the backing fabric, cut:
- ➡ One 38" x 38" square

From each of the Inchie fabrics, cut:
- ➡ One 2½" square for Inchies (total 16)

From the filler, cut:
- ➡ Four 5" squares

From the stiffener, cut:
- ➡ Four 5½" squares

Make the Quilt
Piece the units

Make a unit of an A and B piece and another unit of an A and C piece (fig. 1). Begin sewing at the straight edges, and stop at the dot and backstitch. Press the seam allowances toward piece A.

Join as shown, matching the dots and seams. Press seam allowances toward unit A/C. Make 4.

For the center unit, arrange pieces C, D, E, and F as shown (fig. 2). Sew pieces C to pieces D and press the seam allowances toward D. Join the remaining pieces in rows and sew the rows together, pressing the seam allowances in opposing directions.

Sew a unit 1 to each side of the center unit, matching seams and dots (fig. 3). Press the seam allowances toward unit 1.

Sew a piece B to each side of unit 1, matching the dots (fig. 4). Press the seam allowances toward unit 1.

Assemble the quilt center

Lay out the quilt (fig. 5) and sew the rows together. Press the seam allowances outward.

Add setting pieces G, sewing the inside straight-grain seam first, and then sewing the bias edge of each piece G to piece B, matching the dots.

To sew the miters between G pieces at the corners, fold the quilt top in half diagonally as shown (fig. 6) and match the dots. Start stitching at the outer corner and stop at the inside dot and backstitch.

Add the borders

For each side of the quilt, sew the border strips together into one unit. Press the seam allowances toward the outer borders.

> **Tip!** Be sure to transfer the dots from the templates to your fabric. When joining these pieces, start sewing just ahead of the first dot, backstitch to the dot, then stitch the seam, stopping at the second dot and backstitching.

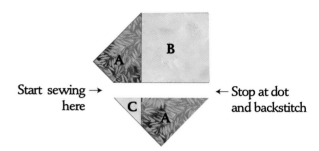

Start sewing → here

← Stop at dot and backstitch

FIG. 1. Make 4 unit 1.

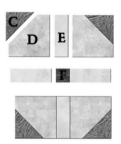

FIG. 2. Make 1 center unit.

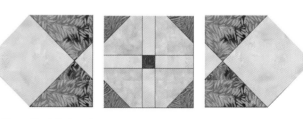

FIG. 3. Make 1.

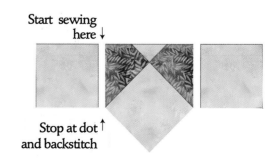

Start sewing here ↓

Stop at dot ↑ and backstitch

FIG. 4. Make 2.

Attach the borders as a unit to each side of the quilt and miter the corners, as shown on pages 34-35, matching the border seams.

Quilt and finish

Layer the quilt with batting and backing. Quilt as desired. Use your favorite binding method to bind the quilt with the 2½" strips of the binding fabric.

Make the Inchies

Make four Inchie sandwiches. Arrange four of the 2½" Inchie fabric squares on the filler, stiffener, and backing, keeping fabrics of similar colors together on each sandwich (fig. 7). Refer to the Basic Inchie Instructions (pages 12–20) to make 64 colorwash Inchies, four from each of the Inchie fabrics.

Embellish the Inchies with beads, wire, decorative threads, crystals, or found objects as desired. Refer to Making Them Stick (page 17) to attach the Inchies with Velcro, positioning them as shown in the quilt photo. Mix up and arrange the colors as desired. You will have seven Inchies left over. Attach them on the back with extra pieces of Velcro, or set them aside for use in other projects or swaps.

DIMINUTIVE DETAILS

The Colorwash Inchies on this quilt have a wide variety of embellishments, including fusible ribbon, colored copper wire, beads, and Swarovski hot-fix crystals. The color and value of the embellishments blend well with the Inchies for a subtle, yet striking, effect.

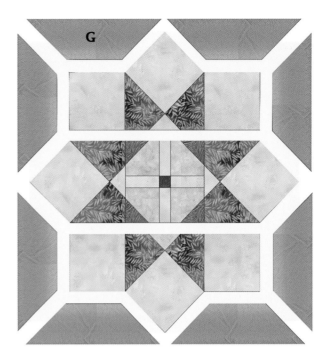

FIG. 5.

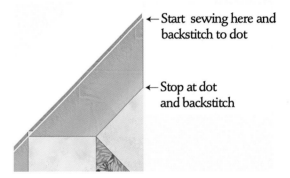

← Start sewing here and backstitch to dot

← Stop at dot and backstitch

FIG. 6.

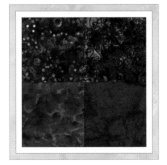

FIG. 7.

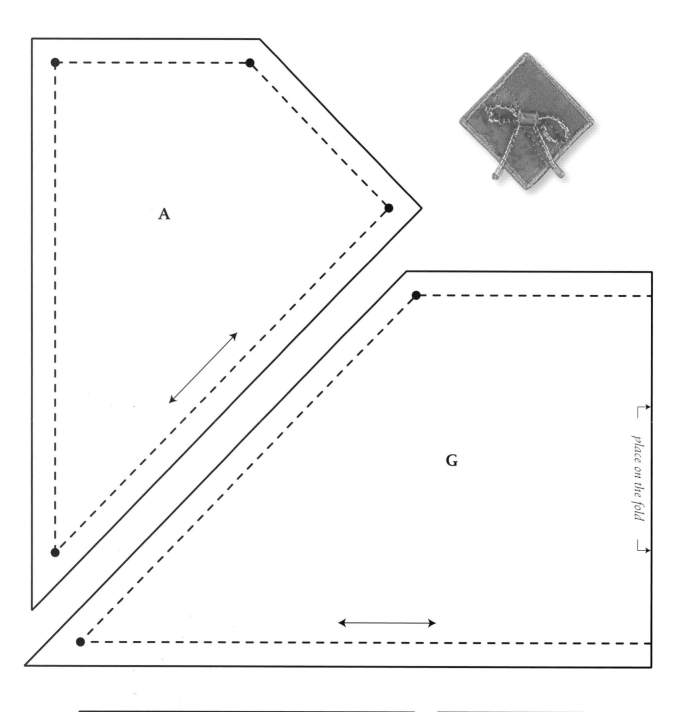

A

G

place on the fold

E

F

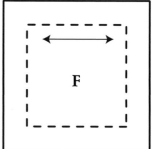

Tip! Cut fabric pieces carefully and mark only the dots shown on the templates. These are the dots you'll need while piecing to ensure the points and corners match properly. For piece G, position the template on the ombre fabric to highlight the colors you wish to see, and cut eight pieces exactly the same.

B

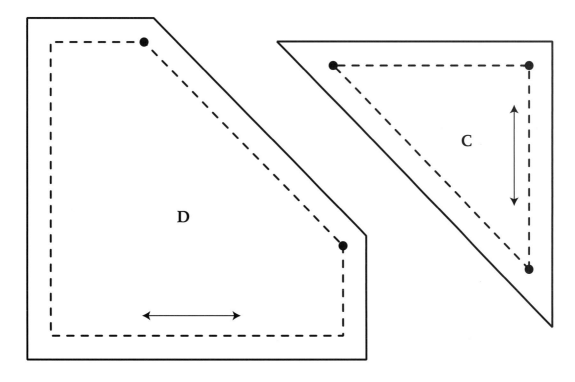

D

C

Resources

Montano, Judith Baker. *Elegant Stitches: An Illustrated Stitch Guide and Source Book of Inspiration.* C&T Publishing, January, 1995

Stori, Mary. *All-in-One Beading Buddy.* C&T Publishing, December, 2007

Van Horn, Larkin Jean. *Beadwork for Fabric Artists.* Larkin Jean & G. Armour Van Horn, March, 2004
and
Van Horn, Larkin Jean. *Beading on Fabric: Encyclopedia of Bead Stitch Techniques.* Interweave Press, September, 2006

Sources

Cheri's Crystals
(940) 497-6399
www.cheriscrystals.com
   Swarovski® hot-fix crystals; hot-fix heat tool, trays; tweezers

C. Jenkins Necktie & Chemical Company
39 S. Schlueter Ave.
Dellwood, MO 63135
314-521-7544 ext 22
www.cjenkinscompany.com
   Bubble Jet Set 2000® and Bubble Jet Rinse

DreamWeaver's Quilts
848 N. Rainbow Blvd. #2022
Las Vegas, NV 89107-1103
www.shop.dreamweavers-quilts.com
   Freudenberg/Vilene® S520 Stiffener and HH650 Fleece; InchieSee

InchieDo Viewer Tool and Ruler set; Microtex/Sharp needles, hand sewing and embellishment needles; YLI Soft Touch Cotton 60wt. bobbin thread, C-Lon® beading thread; bead mixes

eQuilter
5455 Spine Road, Suite E
Boulder, CO 80301
(877) 322-7423
www.equilter.com
   Hobbs Thermore® polyester batting; Pellon® Peltex interfacing;

Kimberly Einmo
www.Kimberlyeinmo.com
   Easy Star & Geese Ruler

King's Men Quilting Supply, Inc.
2570 N. Walnut (location)
P. O. Box 362 (mailing)
Rochester, Illinois 62563
(217) 498-9460
www.kmquiltingsupply.com
   Hobbs Thermore® polyester batting

Kreinik Mfg. Co., Inc.
1708 Gihon Road
Parkersburg, WV 26102
(800) 537-2166
www.Kreinik.com
   Adhesive Teflon® Press Cloth

Nordic Needle, Inc.
1314 Gateway Dr. SW
Fargo, ND 58103
(800) 433-4321
www.nordicneedle.com
   Weeks Dye Works hand-over-dyed embroidery floss, silk ribbon

Quilting Warehouse
(831) 768-4200
www.quilting-warehouse.com
   VELCRO® brand Fabric Fusion® tape; Hofmann Originals bead mixes; fibers and fiber mixes, needles; fabric glue; fusible web; Easy Star & Geese Ruler
   VELCRO® is a registered trademark of Velcro Industries B. V.

Red Rock Threads
150 S Hwy 160
Suite C8-298
Pahrump, NV 89048
(775)751-9972
www.redrockthreads.com
   Floriani Heat N Sta® Fusible Fleece; Sulky® 40-wt. rayon thread; Aurifil® thread

Sewing Supply Warehouse
1900 Tamiami Trail, Unit 114
Port Charlotte, FL 33948
(941) 766-7118
www.sewingsupplywarehouse.com
   Sulky® 40wt. rayon thread

Soft Expressions
1230 N. Jefferson Street, Suite M
Anaheim, CA 92807
888-545-8616
www.softexpressions.com
   Hofmann Originals bead mixes; fibers and fiber mixes; needles

About the Author

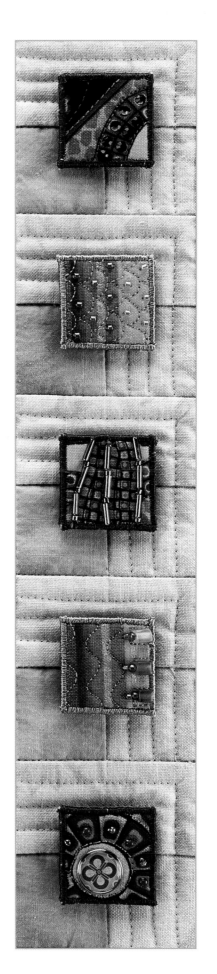

Nadine Ruggles has been sewing and crafting since childhood and caught the quilting bug in 1990. She wanted to make "just one (large) quilt" for the bed and, of course, couldn't stop quilting after that. Being mostly self-taught, she sees each new quilt as a challenge and combines her special talents for fabric selection, precision piecing, elegant quilting, and unexpected embellishments to create innovative quilt art pieces.

She enjoys choosing fabrics, finding the perfect fabric for a certain block or pattern, and putting different colors and fabrics together to create new effects. Her work is a collection of many styles; some quilts are decidedly traditional, while others are more innovative or in the art quilt genre. Quilts and projects with many different fabrics are the most interesting and challenging to her.

Nadine lives in Angelbachtal, Germany, with her husband Eric, who works with the US Army, and two beautiful daughters, Erica and Erin. Patches and Shadow, the family cats, keep her company in her quilting studio. She teaches classes and workshops in a variety of quilting and embellishment techniques for the Army Arts & Crafts programs, as well as for local quilt guilds and shops. Her quilts have been exhibited across the United States in quilt shows, galleries, and museums.